AIRBNB FOR BEGINNERS MADE EASY

Quick Start Guide to Secure Listings, Simple Legalities,
and Profitable Returns in 30 Days or Less

QIVIST PUBLISHING

Table of Contents

Introduction

Buying a house is one of life's greatest achievements, and no one forgets the intense emotions of accomplishment and joy that you feel when your house keys get handed to you. From locations and credit scores to budgets and deposits, the journey of acquiring a house is tedious and stressful but, as Suze Orman once said, "Owning a home is a keystone of wealth—both financial affluence and emotional security" (Carroll, 2023).

As your knowledge about financial stability and wealth begins to grow, you see the importance of identifying assets from liabilities. Unfortunately, not many of us have more than $100,000 lying around to spend. So, many of us are left with the option to acquire a house with the help of a home loan. But look what happens—when you buy a house for your personal occupation, it turns into an asset that requires potentially expensive updates and maintenance over time. Being able to create an income-producing asset out of something that can feel like an expense is when people like yourself begin exploring alternatives. From running a business at home and getting a loan against your house to flipping properties for reselling and renting your property through long-term agreements, there are numerous options you can try to turn your home from a liability to an asset.

Airbnb Is the Answer

Listing properties with vacation renting companies is pretty popular among homeowners who are looking to earn an additional income. These online marketplaces connect homeowners with people who wish to rent out a property, usually for a short period of time. For travelers, this is an affordable alternative to hotels that are often expensive, but for homeowners, this is a lucrative opportunity for you to make money off your property without needing to build an entire hotel or bed and breakfast to do so.

Airbnb is a popular vacation renting company that many homeowners and renters trust. It's easy to use for all parties, cost-effective, and certainly a home away from home for many.

Unfortunately, because this way of earning additional income for homeowners haven't been around for longer than a decade, many people are either skeptical or overwhelmed by the idea of joining a venture like this. But don't worry—you're in safe hands because I'm here to help.

I've been fortunate enough to meet and interact with many hosts who have joined Airbnb, and truly speaking, people join for all kinds of reasons. Some people join Airbnb because they've always dreamed of owning a hotel or bed and breakfast but couldn't achieve this for whatever reason. Some join due to financial obligations that force them to sell their property or make money from it. Others join because they have additional space that they feel can be used to make some extra money. The reasoning will be different for each of us, but what's important is to understand that your choice to start an Airbnb business doesn't have to be as complex and formal as you may think it is.

We'll get to talking about the pros and cons that come with joining Airbnb as a host shortly; however, one of the reasons so many hosts appreciate the platform is that it offers a flexible and fun way for homeowners to meet customers. It offers a business model that helps many of us achieve our goals and guests can find the perfect space according to their location and various preferences. It's a win-win for everyone!

The Good, the Bad, and the Ugly

Real estate is a great way to generate passive income, but as with everything in life it does come with its fair share of ups and downs. Therefore, as a beginner, before you start answering questions centered around figuring out where to begin, you need to ask yourself, "Is this for me?" after thoroughly assessing the pros and cons that come with venturing into real estate and hosting on Airbnb.

The Good

Let's start by listing some of the main benefits that I and many Airbnb hosts enjoy (Brown, 2023):

- The platform offers hosts an easy and quick opportunity to generate additional income. By catering to an extensive range of rental units, private villas, and luxury resorts, even the most basic accommodations have a chance to thrive in the industry.
- You don't need training, qualifications, a special course, or an in-depth guide on how to join the platform. Listing your property is straightforward. To make transactions quick and simple, the platform offers automated payment systems to make the experience convenient for everyone.
- Although you're renting your property out to tenants who are looking for a short stay, not being tied to long-term lease agreements will allow you to maximize profits.

The Bad and the Ugly

Let's look at some of the challenges that you could face when you list your property on Airbnb (Brown, 2023):

- Every booking will come with a charged commission. This will reduce your profits, especially if you have long-term rentals or several rentals. At times, you may feel the need to charge a higher rate or include cleaning fees that will help offset this commission.

- Because the platform offers convenient and affordable places to stay, you may attract guests who won't show much regard for your property and amenities. The good news is that you can always make use of Airbnb's AirCover for hosts to address this concern.
- Because Airbnb doesn't run background checks or proper filtering on guests, you may be vulnerable to scammers.

With the right precautions, coverage, and knowledge of Airbnb, you can always find ways to navigate around the pitfalls that come with entering this world. When you finally have a hold over these nuances, you can definitely look forward to more enjoyable experiences with the platform while reaping rewards from your profitable investment.

To Be or Not to Be? That Is the Question

By now, I'm sure hundreds of thoughts of excitement and concern continue to flood your mind but rest assured that this is perfectly common for any beginner. From personal experience, I've seen that four main pain points stand out when you consider this venture:

- You feel you need more information to help you decide on whether or not you should become an Airbnb host. You lack the confidence and knowledge you need to navigate the platform. This sparks concern over offering and managing your property. As a result, you need a guide to qualify yourself and show you how to use and get the most out of the platform.

- You lack insider access or understanding to determine how much you'll take home. You don't know how to price your property to ensure you don't lose money.
- You feel uneasy about having strangers stay at your property. You want to know how you can list your properties without the risk of spending money on repairs and renovations.
- You need help making your property appealing. Furthermore, you need guidance on how to communicate effectively with potential customers.

Different resources and books will offer you different solutions to each of the pain points listed above; however, I've found complete reward and satisfaction from a method known as the QUEST Method. Simply put, this solution means that you will take the time to do the following:

- **Q**ualify yourself
- **U**nderstand legal aspects
- **E**xplore the market
- **S**et yourself apart
- **T**ake it to the next level

With this method, you'll be able to determine if becoming an Airbnb host is for you, understand the taxes and laws surrounding short-term rentals, discover how to analyze the market to understand the needs and wants of guests, market your listings and make them appealing to potential guests, and implement strategies to take your business to the next level.

My goal is to help you gain the knowledge and confidence to start your venture as an Airbnb host, manage your listings, and become a successful Airbnb host. With valuable and structured content, I've made the book beginner-friendly enough to carefully take you through each stage of your learning phase. Here, you'll find everything is centered around these four points:

- **Understanding the basics of Airbnb hosting:** You want to learn the fundamental concepts of Airbnb, such as setting up a listing, understanding Airbnb's policies, and knowing what to expect as a host. This knowledge forms the foundation for their Airbnb journey.
- **Learning how to optimize listings for maximum visibility and attraction:** You wish to discover techniques that will make your listings stand out. This includes effective photography, compelling descriptions, and competitive pricing strategies. This can lead to increased bookings and higher revenue.
- **Gaining insights on providing excellent guest experiences:** You want tips on how to provide outstanding hospitality, from creating a welcoming space to responsive communication. We all know that happy guests often lead to positive reviews, which are crucial for success on Airbnb.
- **Understanding legal and tax implications:** As a beginner in Airbnb hosting, you need to be aware of the legal and tax considerations involved, such as local regulations, permits, and tax obligations. This knowledge helps you operate legally and avoid potential issues.

- **Learning how to manage bookings and handle challenges:** You'd appreciate advice on managing bookings efficiently, handling cancellations, and dealing with any challenges that may arise during a guest's stay. Here, effective management is key because it leads to smoother operations and less stress on your part.

So, without wasting any more time, let's get into chapter one!

ONE

What Is Airbnb?

In this chapter, we'll start by taking a trip down memory lane and looking at how Airbnb started. We'll also look at its impact on local tourism and other industries to have a better understanding of its model and offerings. As we move along the chapter, I'll be sharing some interesting statistics and fun facts about Airbnb to help show you what makes the platform different and more successful from other platforms of its kind.

What Is Airbnb?

Today, when you see Airbnb as a global marketplace that connects travelers and homeowners who list their homes for rent, know that the founders of the platform, Joe Gebbia, Nathan Blecharczyk, and Brian Chesky didn't enjoy a fruitful and smooth sailing journey from the very beginning because the popular website that's now become a household name today, began with an air mattress, cold floor, and two San Francisco transplants who had nothing to their names and were doing all they could to make ends meet (*Startup Stories - Airbnb: A True Rags to Riches Story*, 2023).

Where It All Began

It's no secret that not every one of us is capable of turning one simple idea into a billion-dollar empire; however, the founders of Airbnb were able to do just that. In 2007, designers Joe Gebbia and Brian Chesky relocated from New York to San Francisco. Back then, aside from hotels, travelers had very few alternatives to explore. So, one weekend, the two designers were faced with a problem because a conference happening in the city had every hotel fully booked with guests; therefore, visitors who booked a little late found themselves in need of accommodation to attend the conference that weekend. This is when Joe reached out to Brian via email saying, "Brian, I thought of a way to make a few bucks—turning our place into a "designer bed and breakfast"—offering young designers who come into town a place to crash during the four-day event, complete with wireless internet, a small desk space, sleeping mat, and breakfast each morning. Ha!"

In a desperate attempt to gather the rent money Joe and Brian needed, they launched a simple website to advertise their bed and breakfast, and this is when Airbnb, which was initially called *Air Bed & Breakfast* scored their first three guests. From that point onwards, Joe and Brian began investing and working on the idea a little more, but their success didn't arrive right away. Instead, because the journey Airbnb was quite rocky at the beginning, they partnered with Nathan Blecharczyk to help them turn the idea into a profitable and sustainable business.

Trials and Rejection

In 2008, Airbnb launched another two times. With the first launch, the company didn't have any luck in attracting new customers; however, on the second try, they managed to attract two new customers. When the summer of 2008 arrived, the Airbnb founders launched the final version of the company's website. This time, the website had been well-thought-out and designed to help guests book their accommodation in just three clicks. Sadly, although this was an incredible milestone, it did come with some disappointments because of the 15 angel investors that all three founders had pitched to; not one of them was interested in the idea. While trying to grow Airbnb that year, the trio remained persistent and resilient to the several rejections they faced. Coupled with that, they also experienced great financial turmoil and mounting debt.

When the 2008 Democratic Convention event took place in Denver that year, the founders hoped that the influx of visitors would leave local hotels overbooked, leaving another opportunity for them to fully capitalize on. Unfortunately, things didn't work as planned and instead of hosting guests, the trio decided to sell cereal boxes that they redesigned and priced at $40 each. Thankfully, the idea was a huge success, and this helped them generate an income of $30,000 that they put toward their Airbnb company.

A while after the event, the Airbnb founders met Paul Graham, who is the founder of Y Combinator, which is a prestigious acceler-ator for startup businesses. With his help, Airbnb underwent major development which pushed the founders to refine their approach. As the founders worked on writing reviews for each of their rentals and accompanying these reviews with professional photographs, this led to an official change to the company, hence the name Airbnb in March of 2009. A month after the change, the company landed a capital investment of $600,000, and this was thanks to the American venture capital firm Sequoia Capital.

A Journey of Success

After securing the seed capital from Sequoia Capital, Airbnb's founders invested a lot of their time, energy, and capital in growing and understanding the company. For instance, it's said that Brian Chesky spent the whole of 2010 living in Airbnb rentals for several months. This helped establish the platform in 89 countries across the globe. As a result, the company grew in value to more than $1 billion. It also received more than $112 million in investments. This led the company to become a Silicon Valley unicorn startup, and this simply means that the company was receiving recognition as being a privately owned startup company that was worth more than $1 billion (Chen, 2022).

As an outsider looking in, Airbnb was doing exceptionally well during the years leading to 2020, and because of this, the founders decided to announce their plan to go public with the company. Unfortunately, things began to take a turn for the worse after this because problems began to surface at every given moment. In addition to hosts beginning to complain and report their homes getting trashed by guests, Airbnb started encountering fines, evictions, and even more problems. Eventually, campaigns across the globe began to rally against the company. This was an incredibly challenging time for the company's founders because the company's sustainability and ability to adapt were being put to the test. Furthermore, the founders were tasked with having to find creative ways to navigate these challenges so the company wouldn't sink. Fortunately, because the founders of Airbnb are known for establishing a winning startup idea, they overcame this tough period, and today, Airbnb is a household name that virtually all travelers turn to for their home away from home.

Getting to Know Airbnb Today

Now that we've taken a trip down memory lane, it's time we understand Airbnb's mission, vision, objectives, and business model today. Essentially, the company's modus operandi is that it's a marketplace that connects hosts and guests by allowing hosts to list their homes for rent while guests get to discover these different properties and book a place to stay according to their preferences. Listings can be done by businesses or individuals, but the important thing to note is that Airbnb doesn't own or claim to own these rental properties.

Before Airbnb introduced this *home-sharing* concept to the world, hotels were always the number one go-to for travel accommodation. It's when you are really out of options that your last resort would be a bed-and-breakfast. It's only recently that the idea of having homeowners rent their homes off to strangers or have travelers stay in a stranger's home became a *thing*. Before then, you'd have to be acquainted with the host or guest before concluding such an agreement. Nevertheless, Airbnb has changed the name of the game by becoming a leading travel technology company in the last two decades. Granted, the overall concept of the company was innovative; however, Airbnb continues to reach greater heights due to its ideal timing, global expansion, solid execution, investments, and ability to reinvest profits.

Understanding the Airbnb Model

The Airbnb business model is all about serving guests and property owners as property owners get to list their rental properties or homes while guests get to book their property of choice for a set period. To make money as a company, Airbnb will charge guests and property owners a service fee for each booking that's made and this ranges anywhere between 3% to 14.2% for property owners while guests get charged anywhere between 0% to 20% (IGMS, 2023). All of this will depend on various factors like the price and location of the booking. Additionally, Airbnb also offers added services like photography and cleaning, but this is all optional for property owners.

When it comes to Airbnb's relationship with property owners, the company aims to achieve two things—attract more bookings and optimize listings. With every service that it offers, the goal is to empower homeowners like yourself to become successful small business owners who take advantage of spaces they feel are underutilized. Then, when you think of Airbnb's relationship with guests, the company aims to provide travelers with a diverse selection of choices that will cater to every kind of traveler's needs. Here, everyone is set to win.

The Sharing Economy and How Airbnb Fits Into It

Also known as collaborative consumption or peer-to-peer economy, the sharing economy is a socio-economic system that is centered around sharing intellectual and physical resources. For instance, seniors may choose to permanently relocate to a new home or facility because they're now aging. If the house they own is paid up, they may choose to rent the property out by listing it on Airbnb. There are numerous reasons why people may choose to rent out their properties, but the gist of it all is that sharing economies thrive by capitalizing on technology to facilitate transactions and exchanges between different parties and systems like this often increase convenience and reduce costs for everyone involved in the transaction and exchange.

The entire Airbnb model exemplifies this system so well because it offers guests and hosts a platform to meet each other's needs. Here, hosts get to generate an income stream from their underutilized assets while travelers looking for alternatives to hotel accommodations can find unique and cost-effective options that will suit their tastes and preferences.

The Peer-To-Peer Model

Airbnb works on a peer-to-peer model. This means that hosts will use details like availability, price, the size of the accommodation, and location to list their properties while guests will search and filter their options to find accommodations that will best meet their needs.

Another aspect of Airbnb is its "Experiences" selection which works to offer platform visitors and users different activities led by local hosts. Here, guests will have the option to book these activities as an add-on or separate addition to the accommodation.

These activities include anything from guided tours to cooking classes. Essentially, Airbnb does this to provide guests with local, unique, and personalized experiences that they will certainly enjoy as they travel. It's all a part of the company's strategic growth.

Explanation of the Airbnb Platform: How It Works

When you're a host, this is how you'll go about exploring the full functionality of the platform:

1. With the space that you're planning to rent, you'll list this space on the platform by sharing the property's location, amenities, size, rules, availability, and pricing.
2. After sharing the details, you'll have the opportunity to share photos of the place.
3. After uploading the photos, you'll write a full description of the space, but most hosts use these personal descriptions as an opportunity to make the list more appealing by

discussing the different benefits that you have to renting that space.

4. After listing the space, your property will be visible to visitors viewing the platform from across the globe.

As a guest, this is how they will navigate the platform until they finally choose a space and make a booking:

1. Guests from anywhere in the world will search for accommodation according to factors like the location, specific amenities, travel dates, and the type of property they're looking for, and price range.
2. The platform will provide them with a full list of properties that they can look at based on the answers they provided to each of the factors that the platform lists.
3. The guest will select their favorite property and proceed to contact the host directly by making use of Airbnb's messaging system. They can use this chat option to clarify details or ask questions.
4. To book the space, the guest will make a payment based on the price that's been listed on the site. All the additional fees relating to service fees or cleaning fees will be included in the price.
5. To facilitate the booking, the guest will make use of the platform's secure payment system, and when the payment is successful, Airbnb will release this payment to the host only 24 hours after check-in. This is to ensure the guest arrives at the accommodation and is happy with the property.

To promote respect and trust, Airbnb allows guests and hosts to leave reviews about their stay. Hosts and guests are advised to not take these reviews for granted because they play a crucial role in the decisions that will be made in the future. For instance, hosts may be reluctant and unlikely to host guests who have poor ratings on their profiles for fear of dealing with an uncooperative guest or an individual who doesn't respect people's properties and belongings. Also, guests may be reluctant and unlikely to book spaces that are unsafe, unclean, or far below expectations. They also don't want to deal with hosts who are said to be unresponsive to concerns or complaints and unprofessional.

Airbnb as a Service

The variety of accommodations that Airbnb offers has undeniably changed the travel and hospitality industry because of the wide selection of personalized and unique choices guests have to choose from. Here's a look at the different types of listings that the platform has to offer.

Whole Homes

A whole home is just that—an entire property. Of course, much like having a house of your own, these properties provide guests with complete privacy and spaces that a normal apartment, villa, loft, or house would have. This includes living rooms, kitchens, bathrooms, and bedrooms.

Private Rooms

With private rooms, a guest will rent an individual room within a host's property; however, when it comes to other areas of the space like the living room and kitchen, the guest will share this with other guests who will also be renting private rooms on the property. Sometimes, the guest can share the rest of the property with the host if the host happens to live on the property.

Shared Rooms

With shared rooms, the guests will share every part of the property, including the bedroom and bathroom that they're renting. You may not think much of this type of listing, but many travelers are looking for budget-friendly options, so this type of listing is usually ideal for flexible or solo travelers.

Unique Stays

Some travelers are intrigued by unusual and extraordinary spaces. Therefore, if you happen to own a castle, treehouse, boat, or yurt, you might want to consider listing it as a unique travel experience.

Airbnb Plus

These listings are for homes that are high-quality and well-equipped. It's excellent for guests who are very attentive and particular with their preferences and experiences. With each Airbnb Plus property, the space undergoes inspection and verification to ensure it reaches the design, consistency, and comfort that your guest is looking for.

Airbnb Luxe

For guests who are looking for the ultimate luxury experience, this type of listing is where they'll find them. Airbnb Luxe properties are high-end spaces with top-tier services and amenities that include things like housekeeping services, trip designers to coordinate everything and other personalized services that guests would appreciate.

Airbnb Experiences

Earlier in the chapter, we spoke about Airbnb offering guests a range of activities that they can do while visiting a specific destination. These are known as Airbnb Experiences, and they're designed and hosted by business locals who are willing to do more than just offer a typical workshop or tour experience. These locals go out of their way to provide guests with the opportunity to fully immerse themselves in different worlds, and this offers them a more mean-ingful perspective of the place they're visiting.

But why do this? Well, with Airbnb Experiences, travelers get to explore the unique culture of local tradition. So, the platform can allow guests to take a cooking class with a local chef or hike through hidden terrain with the help of a local guide. All of these activities are there to offer guests unique and personalized experiences that will make their stay unforgettable.

Airbnb Online Experiences

The COVID-19 pandemic brought about massive changes to individuals and businesses. Unfortunately, many businesses were shut down as a result of the pandemic. With travel restrictions bringing many barriers to how things can be done within the hospitality industry, Airbnb adapted to these changes and introduced Airbnb Online Experiences.

With Airbnb Online Experiences, hosts could continue generating an income from their listings because guests still had the opportunity to engage in social activities; however, the twist was that all of this was being done virtually and with the help of video conferencing technology. When Airbnb Online Experiences launched, the project turned into an immediate success. Here, you will find a range of activities to try, like interactive concerts, virtual tours, and online classes. Furthermore, all these activities would still be hosted by locals and experts.

The Impact of Airbnb on the Vacation Rental Space

Airbnb took the hospitality industry by storm when it invented the concept of having hosts rent out their private properties, regardless of whether the residence was a unique accommodation, private room, shared room, or the whole house. When homeowners came to learn about this, they all discovered an opportunity to generate passive income through offering more local and personalized experiences. Additionally, the platform came with highly competitive price points that gave many hotels and bed-and-breakfast establishments a run for their money. So, regardless of a guest's choice of location or type of accommodation, they could find virtu-ally anything they are looking for, thanks to Airbnb's diverse options. These options aren't typically available on your more traditional channels and has caused a lot of disruption in the traditional lodging industry.

The Impact on Pricing and Availability in Popular Tourist Destinations

Airbnb has introduced a lot of competition in the hospitality industry but a lot of its impact on popular tourist destinations. While this does afford travelers more availability and affordable options, it's said that the rise of Airbnb in popular tourist destinations has led to a rise in property prices and a drop in rental availability that's more long-term in certain cities. This means that people looking to rent properties in these popular tourist destinations for long periods are often unsuccessful because property owners feel they can make more money from short-term rentals that Airbnb offers.

Airbnb's Role in the Global Rise of the Sharing Economy

Because of how successful Airbnb's business model has been, the idea behind the sharing economy has become more popular. This was fueled by having the platform show the world how revolutionary business can be when you take an underutilized asset and convert it into a source of income, encouraging entrepreneurs and business owners to think outside the box.

Economic and Social Implications of This Trend

The rise of the sharing economy and Airbnb business has inspired many businesses and industries to learn to use their resources more efficiently, as it has the potential to encourage income growth and diversity. As amazing as this sounds for all those who are interested, the economic and social implications of this trend have raised concerns about topics like the impact all this has on local communities, safety, and the rights of workers.

Fostering Local Economies

Let's look at Airbnb's impact on local tourism and real estate markets.

Airbnb's Impact on Local Tourism

When Airbnb offers visitors unique experiences and accommodations, this encourages tourism in the area. This spreads a great deal of benefit to the tourism industry, and when local hosts promote local businesses to their guests, this helps local attractions, shops, and restaurants make more money.

Airbnb's Effect on Local Real Estate Markets

The relationship between Airbnb and local real estate markets can be pretty complex. While it's true that Airbnb's effect goes as far as making properties more expensive and discouraging rentals in the area, we can't ignore the fact that it can encourage a great source of income for homeowners.

Regulatory and Legal Challenges Faced by Airbnb

Unfortunately, because the Airbnb business model is new, existing laws across the globe aren't designed to support platforms like this. For this reason, Airbnb has faced numerous legal battles that range from property rights and housing shortages to hotel regulations and zoning laws.

While Airbnb is doing all it can to overcome these challenges, this sparks numerous implications for hosts. So, depending on your country, you could face legal challenges relating to legal action and fines if you violate any laws and regulations. As a host, it's incredibly important for you to learn, understand, and comply with the laws in your area to avoid legal challenges along the way.

Thankfully, government authorities are helping platforms like Airbnb by creating new rules and regulations that address short-term rentals. Some of these laws and regulations do enforce existing laws; however, the government authorities are open to the idea of negotiating agreements with the company itself.

With new rules and regulations in place to support platforms like Airbnb this could present some amazing benefits for the business model. For instance, government authorities can increase the limit on the number of days a host can rent out their property. There can also be negotiations for the requirements a host needs to obtain a license. Over time, these regulations and laws can provide a fair and clear framework for the company, helping it operate sustainably and smoothly in the years to come.

In Conclusion

When you have an understanding of where Airbnb started and how its business model is structured, how this benefits you as a property owner becomes more clear. At the end of the day, Airbnb doesn't exist to only benefit itself as a company. By joining the platform as a guest or host, you have lots to gain when it comes to opportunities. So, if you're already sold on the idea of joining Airbnb as a host, it's time you learned about how you can qualify as a host.

TWO

Qualify Yourself

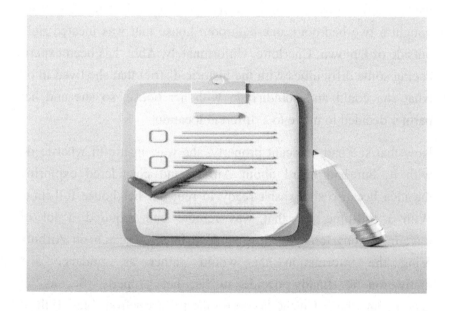

For many years, homeowners have found a lot of opportunities to establish long-term rental agreements with people interested in renting their properties for a month, three months, six months, a year, and even longer. It's a simple and lucrative passive income stream that's turned many homeowners into successful property owners. So, in introducing you to the Airbnb business model, you may be wondering what the difference would be between listing your property on Airbnb and renting out your property with more long-term agreements.

In this chapter, we'll look at the various myths and realities that come with becoming an Airbnb host while determining if you should list your property on the platform and possibly become a successful host.

An Airbnb Success Story

When I started as an Airbnb host some years ago, I met a woman by the name of Abby, and about a year before we had met, she had bought a two-bedroom, one-bathroom house that was located right outside of Uptown, Charlotte. Unfortunately, Abby has been experiencing some difficulties with the historic district that she lived in on what she could and couldn't do with her house, so she and her partner decided to move to a different location.

Now that she had a vacant property, she was unsure of what to do with it, but had heard about Airbnb and considered exploring the idea because she wasn't ready to rent out her house full-time. With a full-time job that was remote and required a lot of traveling, Abby took the time to do a lot of research on Airbnb, using the information she would gather as guidance and motivation to finally decide to list her property. So, as an experiment, she listed the house on the platform from May 19th of that year to September 18th of the same year, and this was done on a full-time basis to see how everything would work out.

When you think of listing your property, you automatically imagine the process to be a complete no-brainer because you'll simply list the property, wait for a guest booking, collect your income, and save, invest, or spend the money. However, like Abby, when you're determined to take this business seriously, you consider things like one-time costs, utilities, and the mortgage. To make sense of all this and ensure she was handling her finances carefully; she put together a spreadsheet that outlined the costs, profits, and overall breakdown of everything involved in her short-term rental business with Airbnb. From reasoning and understanding the market in Charlotte to conclude a listing price and compare the rental value to the Airbnb market, she created a thorough monetary breakdown to detail all the information she needed to run and monitor her business.

After doing her research and creating the monetary breakdown, she started taking advantage of Airbnb's services, and this was something she also advised me to do. One of the services she took full advantage of was the platform's professional photography. When she told me this, I immediately thought, "Well, I'll give that some thought because I can easily do that myself." However, she immediately explained that she preferred the platform's service because the overall quality and lighting were far better. It was after seeing the listing myself that I knew she was definitely onto something.

I admired her honesty and guidance because, with all the effort and consistency she had put in, you'd think her journey was smooth sailing; however, this wasn't the case because she also had her fair share of bad experiences. For instance, she spoke about a time when she had once listed her property as a six-guest house. Of course, most hosts will want to list their property as being able to accommodate many people as this would mean more money on their part; however, after listing the property that way for some months, she decided to change the listing to a four-guest house because there was once a time when her six guests tried to use the house for a party.

While listening to Abby's story, I realized that people resort to joining Airbnb for different reasons, and this reason isn't always the obvious, "I'm looking for an additional way to generate passive income." When you look at Abby's story, you see that she ended up joining Airbnb because she simply wasn't ready to give up on her property due to all the difficulties she had been going through. When she joined the platform, she was doing all she could to get approval for a second-story addition. This resulted in her having to spend large amounts of money on architects, and with one disappointment after the next, she eventually gave up.

When she and her partner moved to a new residence, she still had a lot of furniture that they couldn't take to the new place because it was a little smaller than their first house. So, a vacant and fully furnished house inspired her to join Airbnb, as she felt it was a good way to become a landlord while having full control over her property and making some extra money.

Fortunately, amid the mistakes and numerous learning experiences, Abby persevered, and today, she now generates about $2,000 per month from listing her property on Airbnb. When Abby did her research on how much she would make if she rented the property out, it would have been between $1,200 to $1,700 per month. Of course, there's the part about interacting with guests, maintaining the property, and ensuring the space is clean and safe at all times, but the profit she was left made the experience feel pretty worthwhile, especially because she didn't have to go out of her way to find a tenant, and she was able to choose who stayed at her house.

At the end of the day, joining Airbnb became an enjoyable experience for Abby, especially because she came to love the journey of creating a unique and memorable time for her guests. As a host, she had full control over what she could do to make her listing stand out by offering features and amenities that most listings didn't offer, making it an exciting venture to pursue when you enjoy a good challenge and have a competitive streak in you. Plus, the more she offered, the more enjoyable the experience was for her guests and the more money she made. As usual, it's a win for all.

How Is Airbnb Different From Renting

With a basic understanding of the Airbnb business model and traditional renting agreements, you'd think the only difference between these two options are based on time periods since Airbnb rentals are short-term, while traditional rentals are more long-term. However, there are several key differences between the two.

Differences Between Long and Short-Term Renting

Both Airbnb and traditional renting involve temporary rental agreements that allow renters to occupy a unit in exchange for payment but both these rentals have key differences in their terms and length agreements, tax practices, revenue potential, regulations, and associated costs. Let's discuss this a little further.

Long-Term Renting

Let's look at the advantages and disadvantages of renting out your property through long-term agreements.

Here's a list of the advantages (Park, 2022):

- **A consistent income:** Short-term rentals come with many uncertainties, while long-term agreements provide certainty that you'll receive a consistent income for a set lease period.

- **Less maintenance:** Homeowners are responsible for ensuring their properties are well maintained and this applies to hosts conducting both long and short-term rental agreements. Nevertheless, when it comes to long-term agreements, you have fewer landlord duties to fulfill. Think of it this way—with short-term rentals, you have a new guest occupying your unit every few days. This makes it necessary to perform a day-to-day check on your rental to ensure it's good enough to accommodate a new guest. Of course, screening your tenants thoroughly will be part of your due diligence, but for the most part, the primary responsibility for the overall maintenance of the unit will lie with the renter.

- **Lower turnover:** Ongoing tenancy is an advantage that most landlords can enjoy because having to find a new tenant or guest every few days and weeks will be time-consuming and costly.

Here's a list of the disadvantages:

- **Lower earning potential:** When you take your property and assess the amount of money you'd make on an average nightly rate, you'll find that a traditional rental will typically generate less income than what you'd get on a vacation rental. It's worth noting, however, that the nightly rate you conclude will only apply and be true under the condition that your unit is being booked every day of the week. Unfortunately, this isn't always a reality for Airbnb hosts.

- **Inflexibility:** Many landlords may gravitate towards long-term leases because of their certainties; however, agreements like this may not appear ideal to landlords who prefer not to be *chained* to lengthy contracts.

Short-Term Renting

Let's look at the advantages and disadvantages of renting out your property through short-term agreements.

Here's a list of the advantages (Park, 2022):

- **High earning potential:** When you focus on gross income, you'll see that Airbnb typically yields higher returns. This is because your nightly rate will be considerably more than what you'd find with traditional rentals. However, as mentioned before, this will depend on how often your property is being booked in a month.
- **Flexibility:** As a landlord, you may be a little wary of traditional rental agreements, so the flexibility Airbnb offers with its short rental terms will likely please you. Because Airbnb rentals last anywhere between a night to a few weeks, so it's easy to change your nightly costs. You may not think much of adjusting your nightly rates for now; however, busy periods and seasonal trends do affect your rental income because you may consider reducing your nightly rate during less busy seasons to make your rates a little more competitive. Then, during peak seasons, you may want to increase your nightly rates to take advantage of the high demand. Plus, how can we forget the relief a landlord has when a problematic

guest's term rental is over? With short-term rentals, you'd just need to put up with the guest for the next few days or so. This isn't the case with long-term agreements.

- **No lease agreement:** You may need to one day return or make use of your property for some reason, and if you're fixed on a long-term rental agreement, it may be difficult to end your lease agreement because when a lease is signed, it can only end under specific conditions. These include substantial renovations or a landlord emergency. You'd also need to provide a fair advance notice. With Airbnb, no lease agreements mean less commitment.

- **Built-in insurance:** When you look at platforms like Airbnb, these offer a *host guarantee* that safeguards landlords financially from expenses that they'd need to take care of when there's any damage done to their unit.

Here's a list of the disadvantages:

- **More maintenance:** Because a vacation rental is constantly accommodating a new guest, the property will require constant upkeep. In addition to cleaning the premises for every new guest, like hotels, you're also tasked with ensuring your restock essentials like toiletries and soap. This may prove to be a lot of work for homeowners looking for a passive, yet simple, source of income.

- **More expenses:** Cleaning your property is something you can do to minimize expenses as a host. However, with full-time jobs and other commitments, it is nearly impossible to do this every few days. For this reason, you'll likely consider a cleaning service that you'll pay for on top of the built-in service fees that Airbnb will already be charging. These expenses could take a large chunk of your profits in the long run.

- **The need for furniture and amenities:** With a vacation rental, furniture is mandatory, and while this may not be a problem for some, it could be an additional expense to others. Because many guests are sold based on various amenities like a hot tub or pool, the thought of competing with such could turn many homeowners away.

- **Less stability:** We've already established that a property's nightly income can be higher than what you'd get with traditional renting; however, there's also the possibility of having your property stay unoccupied for some nights and when this happens, you won't make any money.

Airbnb vs. Renting: Rental Income

Let's look at how different rental income is between Airbnb and traditional renting when it comes to pricing, upfront and ongoing expenses, and market and demand.

Pricing

With traditional rental agreements, the landlord has to follow a lease agreement that won't allow them to change rates on the spot. This means that unless the rate changes due to inflation, housing shortages, mortgage interest rates, real estate value, high demands, or the overall market, you'll continue to receive the same rental income each month, and this amount will go in accordance with the rental agreement that's been set. This ensures you have a steady cash flow.

With Airbnb, the option allows you to be a little more flexible with pricing rates. As you venture into the business, you'll develop different pricing strategies; therefore, these strategies will influence the way you'll set your nightly rates when you assess factors like how business is going in a day and how the season and demand are looking.

Upfront and Ongoing Expenses

With Airbnb, the platform requires all units to be fully stocked and furnished. This means that hosts are immediately met with high upfront costs that they'll need to cover to list their properties. When you do finally list the property, you're faced with ongoing expenses that will work to ensure your property meets expectations. Unfortunately, these ongoing expenses don't come cheap because restocking your unit will be something you'll have to do regularly, and you'll always need to replace items that have been stolen, damaged, or broken. Furthermore, collaborating with a property management company will only increase your expenses if you've put them in charge of managing your short-term rental.

With traditional renting, the experience will be a lot different. By finding the right tenant and agreeing to have them take care of the property's maintenance, the only time you'll ever need to step in is when there's an emergency, and this won't be something that happens regularly. Furthermore, you'll be responsible for the proper-ty's general maintenance; however, these are the general responsi-bilities that you face with owning any property like landscaping, painting, building repairs, or pest control.

To put everything into perspective, here's a list of common expenses you would incur through traditional renting:

- garden maintenance
- sewage
- trash removal
- water

Then, here's a list of common expenses you would incur through Airbnb, but it's worth noting that these expenses are in addition to the ones mentioned for traditional renting:

- high-quality furniture
- utilities
- decor
- cleaning services
- bedding
- TV service
- towels
- WiFi
- kitchen utensils
- standard food items like sugar, tea, and coffee
- appliances

Market and Demand

Many people have found a lot of opportunities through platforms like Airbnb, and many have even gone to the extent of purchasing property solely to list it on the platform. As a result, the short-term rental market has been booming far more than your traditional long-term rentals. Now that the pandemic has settled, travel industries across the globe are seeing an upward trend, and this has led to more travelers opting for property bookings on Airbnb. Sadly, the same cannot be said about long-term rentals because the many people who lost their jobs and were heavily affected by the pandemic are still recovering from the financial strain the experience put them through. This has put many of them in a position of wanting to stabilize their finances first before entering into any long-term lease agreement.

As promising as the Airbnb venture may currently seem, it's worth noting that the platform is susceptible to seasonality. This means that during low, less busy seasons, hosts can expect periods of lower income and occupancy. This may discourage some hosts from joining due to the inconsistent rental income; however, there's still an upside to look forward to when the high season arrives. With peak seasons, you can expect short-term rentals to generate the most money due to increased rates and a higher turnover.

When it comes to demand, hosts should exercise a bit of patience because, considering the competition, your property won't boom overnight. To gain attention and come highly recommended, you first need to receive a few five-star ratings before getting more bookings. So, to get your property recognized, you may want to consider offering a discount on your prices, as this is the most effective way to get booked.

Airbnb vs. Renting: Legal Rules and Regulations

Airbnb may be in its booming era; however, regulations against it are on the rise. This makes it incredibly important for every host to do their research diligently because short-term rental laws will vary from one state to the next, making it a slight challenge to get through.

If you're fortunate enough to be in a city that allows short-term rentals, you should try finding out if you will need a permit to run the business. If applying for a permit is necessary, it's worth noting that this will come at an additional cost to you. As an experienced Airbnb host, I wouldn't advise any host to skip this step because if you get caught, you could get fined, or worse, pay for legal action. Also, if you own property in a gated community or apartment build-ing, you may need to get permission from the Homeowners Associ-ation (HOA).

Short-term Rental and Traditional Rental Tax Considerations

Different tax implications come with joining Airbnb. For instance, in the US, depending on the type of rental you own, you're respon-sible for paying state and federal income tax. By listing your prop-erty on Airbnb, you'll also be liable for paying occupancy tax.

Tax is something all homeowners in the rental business can't run away from because even traditional rental income is taxed. Fortu-nately, you're allowed to deduct expenses relating to your property from your tax, but to get the best guidance on how to go about it, a professional tax consultant may be the best person to speak to.

Vacation Rental vs. Traditional Rental Property Insurance

Vacation rental companies often offer property insurance to hosts as a way to protect them by financially reimbursing homeowners in the event of theft or damage. Each platform will differ in how far it's willing to protect hosts, but with Airbnb, hosts are partially protected from theft and damage through the platform's Airbnb Host Guarantee. As relieving as this may appear, it's worth noting that sometimes, this coverage isn't enough, and it's up to hosts to ensure they have additional property insurance.

Property insurance is always a responsible move to make as a homeowner; however, because short-term rentals mean that you'll constantly be hosting different guests throughout the year, your property is at a greater risk of getting damaged. It's this reality that will cause your insurance expenses to be costly.

If you happen to venture into traditional renting, your property insurance will come in the form of a commercial insurance policy or other type of landlord insurance.

Airbnb vs. Renting Factors to Take Into Account

After discussing all the pros and cons that come with long and short-term rentals, it's time we look at the various factors you need to take into account as you work on making your final decision.

Market Rates

Before deciding whether to venture into Airbnb or traditional renting, you need to find out what the average rent prices are in your area for both rental types and compare them. You need to remember that travelers don't travel to every area of the world; therefore, some areas may be far more popular for travelers than others. Depending on your area's market rates, you can explore the option that makes you the most money.

Location

When it comes to considering your property's location, you need to ask yourself if the demand for short-term rentals is adequate for you. You also need to find out if this demand is consistent or seasonal. If your rental property is in a quiet and less frequented place for travelers, it may make sense to opt for more long-term rentals, and if your rental property is in an area that's often visited by travelers, it would make sense to consider listing it on Airbnb.

The Condition of Your Rental Property

By already discussing all the upfront costs that come with ensuring your property is good enough to list on Airbnb, you have to decide on whether or not it's good to list on the platform. If the upfront costs, furnishings, and additional costs will be too much to bear, then perhaps it would be better to consider traditional renting as you may find it difficult to get your property to stand out on the platform. Otherwise, you can consider renovating your old property if you feel it lacks the "wow" factor.

Legal Legislation

Before even considering the Airbnb route, you should make 100% sure that vacation rentals are allowed in your area. If the property is a gated community or apartment building, you need to contact the HOA to find out if it would be acceptable for you to run a rental business there. As lucrative and known as short-term rentals are, it isn't uncommon for states, cities, and associations to deny these kinds of agreements. For this reason, make sure you double-check this to ensure you aren't breaking any laws and rules. Also, if a permit is needed to run the business, be sure to apply for one before hosting guests.

Workload

Although rentals are regarded as passive income streams, they do require some amount of time and effort from your side. So, ask yourself, "How much time can I afford to spend on my rental business?" With long-term rentals, yes, you spend a lot of time arranging lease agreements and screening tenants, but this is something you'll do once or twice a year, depending on how long the lease agreement is.

On the other hand, short-term rentals require a lot more time and effort because finding guests will need marketing. You'll also need to ensure your property is always maintained. With a busy life and schedule, this can be very time-consuming, and that's when hosts resort to collaborating with property management companies. This can be incredibly helpful, but it will come at an extra cost.

The Bottom Line

If all goes well and your property just so happens to be in the perfect location, Airbnb can be a highly lucrative venture that will generate a high return on investment for you. While it wouldn't be practical to hope and assume your property will be booked every night of the year, using the factors and weighing the odds will help you get a more realistic look at what you can expect, and this will help you make the right decision.

If your property doesn't appeal to the short-term rental market for one reason or the other, don't beat yourself up about it. Instead, consider traditional renting and delight in the stability and consistency that will come with this kind of rental option. While the return on investment won't be as high as that of a profitable Airbnb venture, this passive income stream can provide peace of mind to homeowners who are constantly worried about breaking even.

Hosting Myths and Realities

Now that we've unpacked all there is to know about Airbnb, its business model, pros and cons, and how it compares to other popular platforms of its kind, it's time we clear the air about the different myths people often spread and believe about hosting. Here are five common misconceptions that often influence a host's decision to either pursue or leave short-term renting ventures.

Hosting Is Easy

With short-term rental platforms like Airbnb, hosts have enough room to increase their revenue; however, we shouldn't be oblivious to the fact that becoming a successful host will require a great deal of time, consistency, and effort. Also, considering all upfront and ongoing costs, as well as the strict requirements that each of these platforms have, there's a lot to be mindful of when you become a host.

When you manage your business, there's more to it than collecting rent and ensuring your property is clean. You still have guest communications, reviews, and various scenarios that you need to handle. Think about how many requests and questions you'd go through each day just to conclude a single booking because not all communication will guarantee a successful booking. Think about how a single bad review can affect your overall listing profile. Think about the times when you'll need to deal with a guest complaining about a clogged sink or minor leak. Think about scenarios like having to address an issue where your guest has accidentally locked themselves out of the unit. These are all examples of scenarios and events that could happen now and then. Let's also not forget that managing your business will also involve you creating and optimizing your listing through marketing and pricing. You're responsible for juggling all of this on a day-to-day basis.

You Can Make a Lot of Money

The facts and insight I've presented to you so far continue to prove that hosting on the platform can be financially rewarding. Unfortunately, the reality of it all is that this won't be entirely true for all hosts because the big bucks don't come flooding in overnight. Building a steady income will require some time and effort since the income you make is dependent on various factors like your commitment, location, pricing strategy, and property type. Therefore, to make this a worthwhile investment, you'll need to set realistic expectations and apply smart management and dedication.

Airbnb Is a Get-Rich-Quick Scheme

Get-rich-quick schemes are a form of financial fraud; however, when people regard Airbnb as a get-rich-quick scheme, they see it as a legit business that appears like a Ponzi scheme simply because there's often an unspoken promise attached to it which states that "with a small investment and little time, skill, and effort, you can receive a high return on investment because it offers no risk."

Hosting on Airbnb is the complete opposite of all these points because upfront costs alone make you realize that a somewhat large investment is needed to thrive on the platform. To grow on the platform, you will need the skill, time, and effort to reach that point. Also, the venture is risky because you aren't guaranteed a high return.

Only time and a bit of trial-and-error will grow your experience and skill in the rental property game. As a result, even getting the profits you're looking for will take time and a great deal of consistency in providing each of your guests with an exceptional experience. You'll also need to be quick to adapt to the different market changes while ensuring you maintain your property to the utmost guest satisfaction. So, to develop a more realistic approach to this, it's best you set realistic expectations and see this as a long-term investment instead of a project you're pursuing to get a quick buck.

It's All About Location

Finding that your property is located in a high-demand area for short-term rentals is ideal; however, if you plan to purchase more properties with only locations in mind, you may be misled about what actually gets business in Airbnb. According to research, 20% to 30% of your success on the platform comes from listing your property, marketing, and optimizing it daily. So, for example, the photographs you upload will have a direct impact on how your property will perform. If you upload poor to average-quality images, your prospective guests will think they're in for a poor to average-quality experience. However, if you upload professional, high-quality images, your prospective guests will think they're in for a good experience. With better expectations of your property, this will increase your revenue and nightly bookings.

Something else worth noting is dynamic pricing because this can affect your property's returns. When you join Airbnb, you may apply static pricing to your listing; however, you may see an increase in revenue when you convert this strategy to dynamic pricing. This, coupled with what we just mentioned here, all play a crucial role in how your property will perform, further proving that location isn't the only factor to consider.

Hosting an Airbnb Is a Hobby

Hosting on Airbnb doesn't have to be a full-time venture. You can also do it part-time and seasonally. Depending on how you view the business, you can turn this into your primary source of income or a *hustle* that you're running on the side. Either way, it's important to accept and view this as a business. This is because you're paying taxes, are liable for violations, and have to follow local, federal, and state regulations. So, while the venture can be fun and flexible, it's still a business because the law considers it to be one.

Different Hosting Options

Joining Airbnb isn't limited to renting out your space. As a host on the platform, you have the option to pursue any of the following:

- Renting Your Space on Airbnb
- Becoming a Co-Host
- Hosting an Experience

Airbnb Host Requirements

Depending on your goals and preferences, you can explore any of the different hosting options on Airbnb. The important thing is to make sure you meet all of the following requirements:

- respond to inquiries
- accept requests
- avoid cancellations
- maintain a high overall rating

Interactive Element: Are You Qualified?

With everything we've discussed in this chapter, all of it boils down to whether or not you're convinced hosting on Airbnb is for you. To help you make that final decision, here are some important questions you should ask yourself with the help of our "Yes or No" assessment.

Your "Yes or No" Assessment

Here's a quick assessment for you to take. To remember your answers, you can simply tick the box and view your results at the end of the assessment. Please answer these questions as honestly as possible.

Question	Yes	No
Do I have the space?		
Am I comfortable with strangers in my space?		
Is my location desirable?		
Do I understand local regulations?		
Can I handle the responsibilities of hosting?		
Is my property well-suited for guests?		
Am I willing to invest in quality furnishings?		
Can I provide a unique experience?		
Do I have good communication skills?		
Am I financially prepared?		
Do I have a contingency plan?		
Am I open to feedback and improvement?		
Can I handle the unpredictability?		
Do I enjoy meeting new people?		
Is this a short-term or long-term commitment?		

If you answered "no" to one or two of the questions above, perhaps you can work on putting certain measures in place to ensure this venture will work for you. However, if you answered "no" to three or more of the questions above, maybe you should consider putting the idea off for a time you'll be more prepared for or opt for traditional renting if you're truly keen on joining the game. If you answered "yes" to all the questions above, then congratulations because you'll definitely enjoy hosting your space on Airbnb.

In Conclusion

While it's beneficial to you to know all there is to know about Airbnb, it's also good to compare it to other options that may also be of interest to you. Comparison doesn't mean pinning variables against each other to leave one option for the "best one." It also means seeing what other options have to offer to enlighten you on various things you could explore and incorporate into your present choice so it improves your overall experience. For instance, Airbnb already has property insurance that it offers its hosts. If Booking.com offered cover that appealed to you more, this doesn't mean *ditching* Airbnb to hop on Booking.com. It simply means that you'll consider getting additional coverage on your property insurance to ensure you're properly covered for theft and damage.

If you're 100% convinced that Airbnb is the platform you're ready and eager to join, then it's time we get into the next chapter of the book, which will discuss the legal aspects of the game.

THREE

Understanding the Legal Aspects

W e will now look at the legal aspects behind Airbnb like local regulations, insurance, taxes, and permits. Before becoming a host on Airbnb, you must have a clear understanding of this to abide by your government's laws, avoid lawsuits, and not offend any associations or parties involved in this kind of industry. But aside from offending anyone, understanding the legal aspects of your venture also helps create a solid foundation that you can use to defend yourself in the event of an unfair or illegal event. So, knowing the rules of the game empowers you to not get taken for a ride somewhere along the line.

Check Your Zoning Laws and Local Regulations

At the start of your Airbnb journey, like many others, your primary focus will be centered around profits, marketing, and all the costs you'll be incurring, communicating with guests, and ensuring your prop-erty meets all Airbnb requirements. Very few people take the time to learn about zoning laws and local regulations that relate to them; however, this part of your journey is just as important as everything else you're likely focusing on because one offense could have you facing fines and a lot of trouble.

Studying the various laws and regulations that apply to you may feel rather overwhelming at first because few people know where to begin. So, this section is dedicated to giving you the foundation you need. If you happen to reside anywhere outside of the United States, I'd advise you to do your research and do as much as you can to learn these laws so you don't face penalties and fines. However, if you happen to reside in the US, here's a look at which rules and regulations apply to you. Always remember that each state will differ from the next, and rules and regulations will change from time to time. Therefore, for more information on laws and local regula-tions, you can check your local government website for updates.

The Basics

The property game can be pretty exciting to join, but before listing your property on Airbnb, remember that you're in the business of providing short-term renting arrangements, and this means there are a few basics that you should be aware of. Here are nine highlights that I believe every Airbnb host should keep in mind.

Check Your Rental Rules for Short-Term Rental Agreements

Before listing your property on Airbnb, check if your city has any specific rules and regulations regarding short-term rental agreements. If you happen to be renting the property you intend to list, check your lease agreement to see if subleasing the property will be allowed because some property owners won't accept such offers and if it's found that you're renting the property out to Airbnb guests, you could be evicted. Also, Airbnb's rules will vary depending on the location you're in since the platform's rules are based on local laws for each city's short-term rental agreements.

It's important to note that home-sharing or Airbnb isn't allowed in all local governments and in areas that do permit short-term renting, laws have been put in place to govern the practice with the help of hotel ordinances, zoning regulations, and business licensing. Thankfully, every host can use the Airbnb help page as a guide on which laws and regulations apply to you according to your location. If you have any more questions, you can consider getting in touch with your local government offices to clarify any questions or concerns.

Getting Your Licenses and Permits

Most North American cities require hosts to obtain business licenses and permits before listing their properties on the platform because according to your local government, you're now a real estate business owner. As you work on obtaining your licenses and permits, keep in mind that these documents will occasionally have different names, depending on where you're based. So, depending on your location, a business license can be called a

- Lodger's tax license.
- TOT certificate.
- Land use permit.

Also, if you're the owner of more than one property, you may need to obtain a license and permit for each property, even if these prop-erties are within one state. All of this needs to happen before you list your property on Airbnb, and to ensure you don't miss a thing, here are some questions you can use to guide you:

- Do I need a license to run an Airbnb business?
- What permits and licenses are required for me to run my short-term rental business?
- What penalties can I face for violating my Airbnb license?

Checking the Rules Regarding Taxes

In some cities, Airbnb is responsible for collecting local occupancy taxes on the host's behalf. However, in other cities, hosts are the ones responsible for ensuring all taxes from the business are paid. You'll need to check your local area's tax rules to learn which rule applies to you.

In some cases, you may need to sign up for a tax identification number so that your taxes are paid on time. As you confirm which rules apply to you, make sure you play your part in paying your taxes so you don't face issues with the government in the future. Here are some helpful questions that you can ask to check and fully understand how the tax would apply to you according to the state and city that you're from:

- As an Airbnb host, how do taxes apply to my rental business?
- Which Airbnb tax documents and forms do I need to submit to comply with the rules and regulations set out to me?
- How do I report Airbnb income on taxes?
- Is there any additional information I should be aware of to stay compliant with my local tax laws?
- Am I responsible for recording my Airbnb income and expenses for tax purposes?
- Which of my Airbnb expenses are deductible when it comes to tax?
- Does Airbnb provide its hosts with tax forms?
- Do I need to collect occupancy tax?

Always remember that Airbnb is a business, and because of this, you need to do your research on Schedule C and self-employment tax. For those who don't know, Schedule C is an IRS form that taxpayers use to report their business income and expenses. If you're self-employed, a single-member LLC, receive a 1099-NEC form, or own a sole proprietor, you will need to use this form to report all the income and expenses that occur in your trade or business. In addition to self-employment tax, a Medicare and Social Security tax is paid by individuals who work for themselves. As a host, you fall under the category of being self-employed; therefore, you are required to pay your estimated taxes every four months and file an income tax return every year. These are all points that you should be well aware of before you venture into the Airbnb world. Otherwise, you may find yourself facing countless troubles with the law and IRS.

Adhere to Safety and Insurance Regulations

After determining the different documents you'll need to bring to your short-term rental business, the next step would be to ensure your property adheres to safety and insurance regulations. Each city will have its own laws and regulations for guests. This includes ensuring that your unit has smoke detectors installed in it ,as well as a fire escape on the property to protect guests from harm when there's an emergency.

Guest safety is very important in the property game, and if your property doesn't happen to meet some of the platform's require-ments on safety and insurance, then you may want to consider renovating the property. Like the general local laws, each city will have its own safety regulations for guests agreeing to short-term rentals and it's important to adhere to these so your guests remain safe and protected when they're in your home. Adhering to safety regulations may seem a bit tedious on your part; however, it's important to remember that when you're required to install things like carbon monoxide detectors, first-aid kits, fire extinguishers, or a well-lit entrance path, all of these are safety measures that work to protect your guests at all times.

Protecting your guests should be every host's number one priority, and in addition to that, you should also invest in protecting yourself and your property by investing in the right insurance. Unfortunately, as a landlord in the business of offering short-term rentals, you may struggle to find the right coverage with a standard home insurance policy because many of these plans don't cover these kinds of agree-ments. Therefore, you may need to consider upgrading your existing plan for additional coverage. If you already have a standard home insurance policy, then you might want to check this policy to ensure it covers short-term rentals. The great thing about insurance is that some companies in this field offer plans that cater specifically to short-term rentals and not just residential property.

Do the Right Thing as a Neighbor

Airbnb always encourages good neighborly relations, and this is a rule you should keep to as well to help ensure the smooth running of your business. One of the biggest problems most neighbors encounter is noise, and because most hosts aren't physically around to monitor guest behavior, it's important to put policies and rules in place to regulate noise levels, especially during quiet hours. In this case, communicating this with your guests will be key.

The fortunate part about Airbnb is that the platform allows you to list your house rules right off the bat, and this immediately lets potential guests know what your expectations are. For instance, you can let site visitors know that you don't allow unreported guests and parties. With a clear list of house rules, you can set clear boundaries and help avoid future misunderstandings. In my experience, here's a list of house rules that I and many other hosts have mentioned on our listings:

- no events
- no parties
- no loud music
- no unreported guests, and all additional guests need to be approved before check-in
- no pets
- please remember to respect the neighbors by keeping noise levels down during certain hours

- no smoking indoors, and if you are a smoker, please do so outside

While communicating with your guests days before check-in, you can remind them to visit the house rules as a way to reinforce the rules before and during their stay. You have the option to communicate all of this through the following channels:

- email
- in-person
- Airbnb messaging system

It's important to note that parties are banned for all properties listed on Airbnb. The platform does check this to ensure you go above and beyond to prevent guest parties and if it's found that guests have hosted a party without your knowledge, you'll need to report this on the platform as soon as possible.

Avoid Overselling Your Rental

When you list your property, while it's good to be as transparent and accurate as possible; you also need to ensure your property stands out from the rest of the competition. To achieve this, you can work on creating catchy titles and detailed descriptions that focus on highlighting the various features and amenities that make your property unique from everything else that's listed on the property.

As a host, being welcoming, kind, and professional is key; however, it will happen that from time to time, some guests may take advantage of this. To maintain a respectful and safe environment, be clear and concise about your house rules, as this will clarify exactly what you expect from them. This would also be a good time to be upfront about various drawbacks that the guest should be aware of, such as stairs without a lift, deliveries only going as far as reception or the community gate, a small bathroom, or a busy street that's nearby. This will help you prevent negative reviews from guests who feel they were misled and not fully prepared for some of the expe-riences.

At the start of your Airbnb journey, you may be tempted to oversell your property, its features, and amenities in a bid to attract business. You're free to make your listing appear as catchy as can be; however, Airbnb has strict and straightforward policies about providing information that's misleading or deceptive. Should they find any of your information to be inaccurate, you will be removed from the platform immediately. So, from the property's photos and list of features to the description and title, all of this needs to be true and meet the guest's expectations.

Learn About the Penalties and Risks That Come With Not Complying

In addition to knowing the rules, laws, and regulations that come with venturing into the Airbnb business, you should be aware of the risks and penalties that come with non-compliance because this can lead to serious consequences that go from local authority fines and penalties to lawsuits from neighbors and unhappy guests. Further-more, let's not forget that the platform can suspend or remove your listing if you're non-compliant, and this could affect your rental business in numerous ways.

Understanding the Role of a Professional Property Management Company

Having discussed all the work that gets done behind the scenes, sometimes you may struggle to manage your rental business because you're too busy, have multiple properties, or live far from where your rental properties are based. When this happens, you can consider collaborating with a professional property management company that will handle every part of the rental process, from managing your listings and interacting with guests, to setting up your profile and maintaining your property or properties. Addition-ally, they can also help ensure that you're always compliant and aren't at risk of facing fines and penalties for one negligent act or the other. Other services you can expect from these companies include assistance on how to do the following:

- Optimizing your listings so they're more visible to site visitors.
- Managing different strategies for pricing to help maximize profits.
- Provide detailed and valuable reports that will help you monitor the progress of your rental business.

Of course, services like these come at a cost; however, many hosts have found peace of mind and enjoyment from outsourcing these companies.

Stay Informed

As an Airbnb host who's looking to make the most of this opportu-nity, you may consider growing your business in US cities like Chicago and New York simply because of the numerous tourists and businesses they attract. Years ago, this would have been a perfect idea; however, in recent years, local governments have passed laws and regulations that work to regulate or prohibit short-term rentals for one reason or the other.

If, for instance, you look at New York, the city is packed with classic hotels that remain the heart of the area anytime locals, tourists, celebrities, and the wealthy come to visit. Because of this, the city's local government has placed limits on short-term rentals in a bid to keep guests away from vacation rental properties and rather opt for classic hotels. This makes it incredibly important to stay informed about short-term rental news; otherwise, you risk making premature decisions that could leave you at a loss.

Short-Term Rental Rules and Regulations

As we've already discussed, the first step to joining the business is to understand how the laws work in the city or state your rental business will be operating. Some states and cities prohibit short-term rentals due to administrative or zoning codes. Then, in states and cities that do allow short-term rentals, you need to register to offer this service and obtain a permit and/or business license before listing your property and beginning to accept guests. At times, some cities and states may only allow certain types of bookings with short-term rentals. In this case, it's clear to see that every local government will differ in how it chooses to enforce its laws and these differences can also go as far as varying in how landlords get penalized for non-compliance as some may, for instance, receive fines, while others may be penalized with a different type of enforcement.

As a beginner, these rules, laws, and regulations may be confusing; however, the platform is working with governments across the globe to clarify what these rules are and how they apply to you. Where possible, Airbnb can handle local occupancy tax by calculating, gathering, and submitting this on your behalf, as each jurisdic-tion will calculate its occupancy tax differently. However, in cities and states where this isn't possible, hosts are advised to learn and review their local laws before proceeding to list their properties on the platform. This is because the moment you accept the site's terms and conditions, you're certifying that you're aware of your local laws and regulations, understand them, and are ready to follow them.

Your Local Laws and Regulations

Because Airbnb is now an industry leader that's taking the market by storm, this is the perfect time for property owners to start and grow their rental businesses. According to research, it's said that by 2023, the US had anticipated its short-term rental market to be valued at $29.09 billion, and by 2033, it's said that it should reach roughly $81.63 billion in value (*Short-Term Rental Market Size to Hit USD 315.18 Bn by 2033*, n.d.).

Simply put, this means that even more younger adults will have the opportunity to own property and generate a rental income from it. It also means that those who intend to invest in short-term rental businesses will be quite impressed with the returns they'll be making on their investments.

As a property owner who is only joining the industry now, you may be concerned about the competition level that puts you at the bottom of the list. This may make you feel like you may need to work hard and long hours to get your property noticed, raising your concerns about when you can expect to grow in the business. The good news is that with how short-term rental businesses are growing, there's more than enough room and opportunity for anyone to join. However, it's worth noting that as the industry grows, so will local regulations that work to govern where and how your business can operate. Therefore, part of thriving in the business means learning and mastering the different rules and regulations that apply to your city and state.

The legal landscape surrounding the business of short-term rentals is constantly changing as new laws and regulations form to accommodate this addition to the hospitality industry. For this reason, each state and city will differ in how it chooses to regulate the business of short-term rentals, making it incredibly important for you to consult your legal advisors and local government websites for information that will relate specifically to you and your location.

As a beginner, finding the information you need can be overwhelming, especially when you aren't too sure of where to begin. Thankfully, I'll be providing you with a general guide shortly, but before we get into that, you need to remember that as you prepare to find accurate information on the short-term rental laws that apply to your state and local city, your resources should include information that applies to your state and local government. Your focus shouldn't be on just one aspect and not the other. With that in mind, you can then follow this general guide on where to find the information you're looking for.

State Government Websites

In some—but not all—states, there is a specific set of rules to govern the business of short-term rentals. Because they apply across the state, residents can find these regulations on the state's official government website. Here, you'll find detailed sections that are dedicated to discussing housing, business licensing, and consumer protection.

Department of Commerce or Business Licensing

When you're dealing with business regulations and licensing, this has to do with the Department of Commerce or a similar department, depending on your state. State websites do well in directing you to these departments, and it's here that you'll find information on what's required of every host to run a short-term rental business.

Department of Revenue or Taxation

Lodging tax or sales tax often applies to short-term rental businesses that are legally obliged to pay taxes. For accurate and up-to-date information on tax obligations and laws that would apply to you, you'll find an outline of this in your state's Department of Revenue or Taxation.

Local Government Websites

It's county governments and local cities that are often in charge of regulating short-term rental industries. Therefore, while searching your local government website, look for sections discussing business licenses, zoning, and housing because this is where you'll find information on topics like restrictions, occupancy limits, permits, and zoning laws.

Planning and Zoning Departments

Short-term rental businesses aren't allowed just anywhere, and this means that you need to do your research on finding specifics as to where they are allowed and which areas are considered zone restric-tions. In this case, the best place to find these specifics would be on websites dedicated to outlining topics related to planning and zoning departments.

County Commission or City Council

Local governing bodies often record their ordinances and meeting minutes to later share on their websites. Everything discussed in these meetings are made available to the public and by reading through these, you can get a valuable amount of information on short-term rental laws.

Visitor Bureaus and Tourism

Some cities and states use their visitor bureau and tourism websites to provide the public with information concerning short-term rental laws since the industry often serves the tourism industry.

What to Remember

As you go in search of information concerning the legalities of the world you're preparing to enter; a great starting point would be to look for a website that your specified city or county would use to share the information you're after. If you don't find any valuable information on your local laws, the next step would be to visit the Department of Commerce and Business Licensing or the state government's official website. Another step you should consider taking is to consult an expert in real estate or a legal professional who's familiar with laws surrounding short-term rentals. Furthermore, you should always keep in mind that rules and regulations can change. For this reason, it's your responsibility to check your local government's website for updates as often as possible.

Your Questionnaire of Other Legalities

As you work through the legalities, your research shouldn't be limited to rules, laws, and regulations. You also need to consider things like depreciation and the limit on your rental losses. Ask yourself questions like:

- What method will I be using to report my rental income and expenses?
- What method will I be using to report my deductible personal expenses?
- How will I report payments to independent contractors?
- How is my net rental income taxed by the federal government?
- How is my net rental income taxed by the state?
- What will my quarterly estimated tax payments look like?
- Which documents will need to be retained?
- When I compare my list of things to repair and maintain against my list of things to improve, which of these can I capitalize on and which of them can I deduct?

After going through all the costs and taxes involved in running your business, the next step would be to focus on insurance and the like. Here, you'll need to research topics like homeowner's insurance and home sharing. After learning this in great deal, you can then ask yourself questions like:

- When does home sharing turn into a business?
- Does my homeowner's insurance cover my Airbnb business?
- What does home sharing look like as a renter?
- What does Airbnb's insurance cover?

AirCover, host damage protection, reimburses hosts amounts of up to$3 million when their property or belongings are damaged by a guest during their stay and they refuse to pay for the damage (*Host Damage Protection - Airbnb Help Center*, n.d.). You also have the AirCover host liability coverage that provides hosts with amounts of up to $1 million when they're found legally responsible for hurting a guest or damaging their belongings during their stay. These are two forms of insurance that you should think about carefully because although they only happen on rare occasions, if it were to happen to you, you don't want to find yourself without any cover. So, as you work on learning these insurance types a little more, remember to find out the following:

- What does AirCover not cover?
- How do I file a claim with AirCover?

In Conclusion

Laws and regulations may be a lot to get through, but you must remember that these rules exist to protect all parties in the event of an unfavorable situation. By studying the laws and regulations that apply to your property's location, you can put measures in place to ensure you're constantly complying with the law and not placing yourself and your business in danger of breaking any rules. The process of acquiring all this research and knowledge will be tedious but I hope that by providing you with a solid foundation of what to expect and guiding you on where to look, this will make the journey a little easier for you. So, now that we've covered the legalities let's start exploring the market.

FOUR

Explore the Market

Now that you know all there is to know about qualifying yourself and understanding the legal aspects behind short-term rental agreements with Airbnb, it's time you tap into understanding the importance of market research. As we delve more into the chapter, you'll learn about the different strategies and tools you can use to turn your business into a complete success while learning the ins and outs of the market.

Airbnb Challenges

By now, you should know that the more popular the Airbnb platform becomes, the more challenges you'll face. So, while it can turn out to be a lucrative business venture, there are some difficulties that you should be aware of, and that's what we'll discuss in this section.

Your Two Greatest Challenges

Competition

With the right paperwork and basics, it's easy for any landlord to join the Airbnb platform as a host. However, to make this a lucrative business, you need to work your way up, and this won't come easy because you're up against hundreds, if not thousands, of other hosts who are also attempting to do the same thing.

With more popularity and acceptance across the globe, more and more hosts continue to join the business, making it harder for many hosts to remain at the top of the platform's ratings. This is because each time a new listing outperforms you, it could be due to the following factors:

- price undercutting
- limited availability
- negative reviews
- poor communication with your guests
- copycat listings

- photo ordering and selection
- house rules
- descriptions
- cancellation policies

When you're faced with difficulties like these, they only move your listing to the bottom, and this could affect your business on a massive scale.

Seasonal Demand for Rent on Airbnb

Local events and seasons always play a significant role in the short-term rental market. Regardless of your location, this line of business will often have its seasons or highs and lows, and this is due to the following factors:

- **Holiday seasons:** When you look at holidays like Easter, Thanksgiving, and Christmas, you'll see that the market for short-term rentals will increase in areas that celebrate festivities.
- **Events:** Think about the story behind Airbnb. It's concerts, conferences, and sporting events that attract many visitors to specific areas.
- **Weather:** With areas surrounding the beach or lakefront, you'll see an increase in demand for such places around the warmer months of the year. The areas that entertain activities like skiing or other winter sports will see a demand for such areas in the cooler months of the year.
- **School breaks:** When students go on their yearly school breaks, families are more likely to book holiday trips, increasing the demand for family-friendly properties.

Why Market Research Is Important

While deciding whether or not you intend to join a certain business venture, you need to do your digging, but with the various Airbnb challenges that a host faces, it can be difficult to predict any esti-mates just off the top of your head. This is where market research comes into play.

When we talk about market research, we don't mean heading to Google and searching "How much money does an Airbnb host generate in New York City?" Market research means gathering a wealth of data which includes the various services, prices, investors, and occupancies that you can use to make an informed decision on the business. Without market research, your business won't thrive because you'll step into it with a very vague and some-times misinformed understanding of how the business works.

Getting your hands dirty and doing all the digging won't be fun; however, this will prove to be worthwhile in the future because the data you collect will offer you insights into whether you should opt for short-term rentals or long-term rentals, what guests in the area are normally looking for, and more. By the time you prepare your listing, you'll know how to make it enticing enough to stand out from the rest of the competition, and that's gold.

Understanding Your Market

To study your market, you first need to know your target market. Every Airbnb host will have a unique experience that makes it their own, and with the help of market research, you can uncover what makes your location different from the next.

The Airbnb platform offers its hosts numerous resources that they can explore to help them better understand their market. In my experience as a host, I've found great value in the Airbnb calculator because it helped me figure out how much revenue I could generate from the average daily rate, city, and duration of the average guest's stay. It's tools like these that you want to rely on because they will help guide you in the right direction.

Identifying Top Listings

When you finally understand your market, the next step will be to go through your area's top listings. While going through each listing, find details that will give you excellent cues on what the guests who visit your area look for. A good example of this would be to look at the amenities and see which amenities guests praise the most in their reviews.

Understanding Your Competitors

Take the time to thoroughly investigate your direct competitors. These are other Airbnb hosts who share similarities to your listing. Especially with listings that are receiving high reviews, constantly booked, and making it to the top of the list, you want to use their details as a guideline to position your listing in a way that will prove to be just as successful. In this case, you will want to keep your eyes on your competitor's prices, reviews, daily rates, and other things that they offer.

Analyzing Seasonality

We've already determined that one of the greatest challenges you'll face as an Airbnb host is seasonality and while we did discuss factors like holiday seasons, events, weather conditions, and school breaks, market research, can help you navigate the drastic effects that often take a toll on your monthly revenue and occupancy rate.

To thrive during peak seasons and survive low seasons, you can use another Airbnb tool that will allow you access to annual data. With this market research tool, you can gather a more accurate understanding of how seasonalities play out in your area. Before using this market research tool, I dreaded the idea of having to dig through all kinds of data; however, with the one on Airbnb, a single look at your browser is all you need because access to this information is easy, quick, and convenient.

Researching Demand

Coupled with seasonality, your market research also needs to include data on what the demand for vacation rentals looks like in your location and different markets. Find out if there are specific events that cause the demand for your area to go up, and in the event of an increase in demand, find out what the average occupancy rates are. When you have a clear picture of how Airbnb demand operates in your area, you can then make more accurate predictions of what to expect with revenue.

Monitoring Trends

In the world of short-term rentals and Airbnb, changes are always happening; therefore, what appeared to work yesterday won't necessarily work tomorrow, and this principle applies to any location across the globe. For this reason, it's important to conduct your market research regularly, as this will help you stay on top of your game when it comes to your competitive abilities.

Understanding Real Estate Trends

Although you're in the business of short-term rentals as a vacation rental host, you also need to know that you're equally a real estate investor. With that in mind, you shouldn't lock your eyes on Airbnb trends alone. Instead, you should also keep an eye on trends occurring in the broader world of real estate. With regular market research, you'll know when the price of properties is either rising or falling and if the market is favoring the buyer or seller. Allow this information to influence decisions you'll be making in the long run when it comes to renting, buying, or selling any properties in your area.

Gathering Data on What Your Guests Prefer

So far, we've centered all our market research discussions on market trends and competition but your data doesn't stop there because you also need to do some digging on your potential guests. Here, you'll need data concerning their demographics, what these potential guests are looking for in an Airbnb property, and which cities they're interested in seeing. The more you know about them, the more you'll be able to cater to their every need, and when you offer more, you will only improve their experience.

Tracking Macro-Trends

Of course, when you're doing your research, you want to gravitate towards trends that provide insight about your specific market. These trends are known as micro-level trends. As informative and useful as these are, you also want to invest in knowing the trends that affect the Airbnb business as a whole. These trends are known as macro-trends.

Because Airbnb is global, you won't know all there is to know about it; however, you should make it a point to learn about global factors that affect the business, including technological advancements, economic shifts, and travel patterns. All these trends can and will eventually affect your business; therefore, by being aware of these trends and how they will soon affect you, you can start making preparations for what's to come.

Asking Your Guests Questions

Your guests are just as important as knowing about market trends and competitors. The moment they conclude a booking with you and stay on your property, they have a first-hand experience of what it feels like to be hosted by you. At times, it may be a bit difficult to read or accept any negative reviews that a guest may share. Misunderstandings and guests who are generally rude or always expecting too much will sometimes leave you disappointed when it comes to their ratings and reviews; however, it's no use denying or dismissing every negative review that comes your way because there's a lot you can take from those to improve the next guest's experience.

With reviews, always see the positive feedback as a sign that you're doing something right, and you can then use negative reviews as a guide on what you can improve. During a guest's stay, you will have the opportunity to communicate with them and ensure they're enjoying their stay. Also, guests will have the option to rate their stay and leave feedback on their experience.

After a guest's stay, try capitalizing on post-stay surveys. You can simply send this through to them and ask that they share their thoughts on their experience. What I love about post-stay surveys is that you can ask detailed questions that will help you get all the details you need regarding your property and hosting service.

If you're wondering where you would even begin to compile a post-stay survey, you can always structure your questions that take them through their overall journey. So, for instance, when a guest arrives at your address, they will need to check-in. After check-in, they will access the property, look around, and either admire or express disappointment over one thing or the other. In this case, you'll structure your survey to appear something like this:

1. How did you find your check-in experience?
2. Was the property clean when you arrived?
3. Were you satisfied with the amenities we supplied you with?
4. Did you feel safe?
5. Did you find it easy to contact the host during your time of need?
6. If there's anything else you wish we offered or could do for you, what would it be?

When asking these questions, the feedback you receive will help shed some light on what you should improve, add, or remove from your property. By making a habit of consistently engaging with your guests this way, you gather the invaluable data you need while making them feel like their opinion matters to you. The more improvements you make over time, the more guests you'll attract. Plus, with guests you've already established a meaningful connection with, this increases the likelihood of them choosing your property again in the future.

Looking at Environmental Factors

As a property owner, you need to study and know the ins and outs of your property's environment. Let's say your property is close to a beach. Conduct your market research to understand how peak beach seasons affect the occupancy rates on your property. The same would apply if your property is close to, for example, a ski resort. When you have a clear understanding of these different environmental factors, you make more informed decisions when it comes to the strategies you'll use for marketing and pricing.

Studying the First Page of Your Airbnb Search Results

With accurate information on your market, take a moment to study each of the listings that appear immediately when you're met with your search results. In most cases, this first page will likely list all the properties that have the highest ratings and bookings. From marketing, all the way to pricing, study each listing's strategies to see what makes each of these properties rank high on the platform.

Tracking Metrics for Future Use

Doing your market research shouldn't be something you only do in the beginning stages of your business just so you get all the data you need, get a quick estimate on potential revenue, and know how to stand out from the competition. As I mentioned before, in the business of short-term rentals, trends, and various factors are constantly changing. Therefore, market research cannot be a one-time thing. You need to monitor your key metrics as often as you can to gather information about things like occupancy rates, guest reviews, monthly revenue, and more. This will help you spot trends right when they begin, leaving you in a favorable position to adjust each one of your strategies accordingly.

Monitoring New Market Entrants

It goes without saying that the market in which Airbnb operates is profitable and dynamic since more and more property owners are joining the business. While there's more than enough room for everyone to get their fair share of the pie, it's important to stay informed of changes and new entrants that are entering the market. A good example of this would be rental arbitrage. You may think you have the upper hand as a property owner because houses aren't bought every day; however, with the introduction of rental arbitrage, people can rent properties from property owners through long-term agreements and then sublet the property on Airbnb. This makes it possible for virtually anyone to establish an additional income stream without the challenges and stress of needing to own a home.

When it's this *easy* for people to join the platform, this does affect you because it means that you're constantly up against fresh listings all the time, and this could have an impact on your occupancy rates and business as a whole. Although every host would need to work their way up to ranking high on the platform, always remember that these new listings are out to as much market share as they can; therefore, they often implement relatively aggressive strategies to work their way up, and this includes providing special offers, drop-ping their prices, and offering unique services. You need to be aware of this so you can make the necessary adjustments and not have these changing market landscapes affect your business to the point where you're right at the bottom of the list.

At this point, you may be wondering how you can work around the challenge of new market entrants. Knowing this may leave you a little disheartened because all business owners want to generate profits; however, when a new listing offers amenities that are similar to yours but at a lower price, you may need to adjust your pricing strategies. Alternatively, if you notice that a new listing is perhaps attracting attention due to a unique amenity, consider introducing this amenity as well.

You'll spend quite a bit of time monitoring new listings to adjust your strategies and identify competition, but doing this isn't only about that. When you track new listings, you're allowing yourself to make the most of your investment by capitalizing on the inevitable reality of all new listings, which is the time it will take for them to finally, get to the top. Regardless of how aggressive their strategies may be, every host goes through this as factors like reviews play a crucial part in helping each listing work its way up. So, when new hosts are building their reviews, use this opportunity to flaunt your reputable status, as guests typically prefer reviewed properties over unreviewed ones.

How to Start Your Research

Research isn't a strong point for everyone, especially because many people don't know where to begin, the different options one can use to gather data, and process various sources of information. Therefore, this section will focus on how to start your research and how you can go about processing it so it isn't an overwhelming experience.

When you do your Airbnb research, keep in mind that this is being done to increase the chances of turning your investment into a complete success because the information you gather will give you a clear idea of what to expect in the business ahead and how your specific listing will perform when compared to competitors around it. As insightful as this may sound, know that the comparisons and analysis you're hoping to get will require a great deal of data.

Thankfully, Airbnb does provide potential hosts with large amounts of data that are publicly available to anyone, and this includes information on the historical performance and analysis of any property that you may be looking at. Therefore, you can use this information in conjunction with other research that you'll conduct independently to make more informed decisions.

Steps to Conduct Your Airbnb Research

The Airbnb platform offers users several market research tools for you to use and all these resources are available online. So, as you work on exploring these tools and conducting your market research, here are four simple steps to follow.

Step One: Find the Most Ideal City to Run Your Rental Business In

Whether you like it or not, your location will influence your return on investment; therefore, try investing in cities that are popular travel destinations for individuals traveling for business and leisure as these locations will come with strong economies, excellent transportation systems, shopping centers, and other key amenities. As you find good cities to invest in, consider factors like Airbnb trends, whether the city's economy and tourism sector have been experiencing steady growth over the years, and what your return on investment will likely be.

I would recommend a real estate platform called Mashvisor, as it's a highly resourceful one-stop-shop for potential hosts like yourself who are on their way to conducting Airbnb market research. Here, you'll be provided with the latest Airbnb analytics and tools for leading US cities, and this includes data on:

- the platform's occupancy rate
- how much the average host earns
- the average cap rates
- the average cash-on-cash returns

Step Two: Study the City's Airbnb Regulations

The more popular Airbnb becomes, the more regulations cities are putting in place to ensure all parties are protected in this business practice. Once you've found a suitable city to run your business in, you need to study how short-term rentals are regulated in that specific city because each city will vary when it comes to Airbnb regulations, and this fact applies to cities even in the same state. In all the market research you conduct, make sure the city you're looking to operate in will support you enough to achieve all your investment goals.

In this case, you'll want to ask yourself questions like:

- How are taxes regulated in this city?
- What policies have been put in place to protect Airbnb guests?
- Does the city support non-owner-occupied rentals?

When you study these regulations, you'll know how they will affect your business, especially in the long run. Try investing in cities that offer more flexible regulations, as cities with the strictest Airbnb regulations could affect your business significantly. Furthermore, knowing these regulations will help you stay on the good side of the law.

Step Three: Do a Neighborhood Analysis

After finding the right city to run your Airbnb rental business, it's time you find an ideal neighborhood within that city. Each neighborhood will offer a different potential return on investment because one neighborhood may be a popular tourist destination while another may not attract as much attention. Therefore, you'll want to do a neighborhood analysis to find a location that will present you with the most investment opportunities.

As you analyze each neighborhood, choose to invest in one that tourists visit the most. When tourists travel, they want their stay to be close to the places they'll be visiting. This includes tourist attraction sites and other places that often come highly recommended like city centers, aquariums, game parks, museums, and beaches. In this case, you'll want to make use of Airbnb's heatmap which is the Mashvisor platform, as this tool will provide you with a quick analysis of the most profitable neighborhoods in your city.

Step Four: Do Your Comparative Market Analysis

When you walk away from doing your neighborhood analysis, you should have a list of some profitable areas that have caught your attention. With this list, you'll use it to do a comparative market analysis that will guide you in choosing your final neighborhood of choice. When we talk about comparative market analysis, this is one of Airbnb's forms of investment analysis, and it involves determining a rental property's value by comparing the property to similar rental properties in the area. This will help you with the following:

- avoid purchasing overpriced properties
- avoid poor real estate deals
- gain knowledge of how similar properties in your local market are performing
- assess local rental rates

How to Research Your Airbnb's Market and Regulations

To begin the research on your market and its regulations, you need to visit your city council and find information on how your city regulates vacation renting businesses. Before setting out to get there, you need to prepare yourself by asking these key questions:

- Does my city have laws that either oppose Airbnb businesses or support them with the help of existing laws?
- What limitations does my city pose on short-term rentals?
- Does my neighborhood or gated community have an association I should be aware of to regulate short-term

rentals?

- Am I up against hotels and other businesses that offer short-term stays?
- What attractions exist in my area?
- Are there any local hosts that I can perhaps create a network with?

How to Process Airbnb Data

Having started your research, it's time you learn where to find your market research data and how you process all this information to help you make more informed decisions relating to profits, expenses, and choosing the right property for your Airbnb listing:

1. Before you focus on the numbers, make sure you study your city's regulations. This cannot be stressed enough because if the legalities make it difficult for you to achieve your investment goals, you'll struggle to manage your business and all the research you would have conducted would be pointless.
2. Create a spreadsheet that will list various details about your listing.
3. Use an Airbnb tool known as AirDNA Market Minder. This tool will allow you to get additional information about every Airbnb listing you may be interested in studying and when you're ready to extract and gather this information, place it all on the spreadsheet you created in step two.
4. With all the information now on a spreadsheet, use the formula 'AVERAGE' to get the document to calculate your findings' average revenue per year. You'll do this for each unit size and also each neighborhood. To make this step a little more effective, I usually separate my listings

according to units that have the same number of bedrooms. If, for example, I'm grouping all my four-bedroom listings, I will place a three-bedroom, two-bathroom listing in a different category to a three-bedroom, three-bathroom listing.

5. Now that you have all the information you need on a spreadsheet for every size unit you're looking into in each area, you need to investigate which unit size and area generates the highest annual revenue and expenses and compare this to the unit size and area that generates the lowest annual revenue and expenses. When you subtract the highest annual revenue from the lowest annual revenue and the highest expenses from the lowest expenses, this gap will guide you on the potential profit range you could make annually. To work this out, you will need to calculate your expenses and the maximum amount that you'll spend on paying for rent or the property's mortgage. Earlier in the book, we already discussed the different expenses an Airbnb host would incur; therefore, you can use that as a guide to figure out your expenses.

6. It's now time to review your comparables, and this means comparing available rentals with listings already on the Airbnb platform to find something either less than your maximum monthly rent or suitable for rent. Avoid taking anything that comes your way because the available homes you're looking at need to be comparable and not significantly different from each other. This means, for example, that you would compare a successful Airbnb listing with a rooftop patio to a property you're looking at that has a large backyard. These two properties are comparable. However, you wouldn't compare a successful Airbnb luxury home with a pool to an average house that

doesn't have a pool. These two properties aren't comparable. Look for common features in successful Airbnbs in the area and compare them to the available houses you're interested in investing in. When you find a comparable property, you can then approach the landlord with accurate knowledge of how much profit you'll be making from the property.

Tools for Your Market Analysis

Let's summarize the resourceful tools you'll need to use to conduct your market research and gather data.

Mashvisor

Among the different Airbnb market research tools I and many investors use, Mashvisor happens to be the best tool for market research. Simply put, the tools aim to help investors like you and me find profitable properties online. Although the tool only caters to the US housing market, if you're in a different country, try researching similar tools that offer a similar service but cater to your housing market.

This tool is excellent for beginners who are starting their vacation rental journey and are looking for some valuable and resourceful data. It offers a large real estate database that covers all 50 states in the US, and the sources it uses to gather this information are reliable as it partners with big names like Airbnb, the MLS, Realtor.com, and Zillow. Furthermore, the information provided is updated regularly, so you never have to worry about being misled due to out-of-date data.

Other services the tool offers include:

- **A property search tool:** With just an address, city, neighborhood name, or zip code, you can use this search tool to find properties easily and view all the active listings in that area. With the help of its user-friendly interface and custom features, you can gather a ton of information from this tool, making it an ideal go-to for finding rental properties on the Airbnb market.
- **The investment property calculator:** With this tool, investors can use actual market research data to perform all sorts of calculations with ease. Thanks to its interactive and highly intuitive system, the tool gives realistic and accurate projections and estimates to perform a property analysis. This will help you make sound and confident decisions as you venture into the business.

AirDNA Market Minder

This tool provides users with an interactive map that shows different Airbnb listings thanks to an algorithm it uses to predict revenue over a year if the property's listing isn't older than 300 days. Each dot represents a listing, and when you click on it, it will tell you all kinds of information about the listing. This is the information you can use on a spreadsheet when collecting market research data. This information can be anything from occupancy rates and average daily rates to lengths of stay and more.

In Conclusion

Market research can be a daunting experience for many, but with the Airbnb line of business, it's crucial for success. Without taking the right steps or being as thorough as you need to be, you risk making many misinformed decisions that could leave you in a serious financial rut in the long run. With the help of proper guidelines and some useful tools that can help you identify needs, demands, and various considerations, you can make accurate predictions and estimates that can set you up for great success. So, with confidence that you're making the right decisions, let's move on to the next chapter, which will focus on setting yourself apart from your competitors.

We Need Your Reviews!

Hello, Future Entrepreneurs!

🏠 Have you ever thought about all the different ways people can make money from their homes? That's what "Airbnb for Beginners Made Easy" by Qivist Publishing is all about. This book dives into the exciting world of Airbnb and how people turn their homes into fun places for travelers to stay and exciting business opportunities.

For many years, people have been renting out their homes for a long time, such as a month or even a year, which helps them earn money regularly. But Airbnb changes things up by letting homeowners rent their places for shorter times, possibly a few days. This can be even more exciting and can help homeowners meet new people as well as create a way to put your house to work for you to earn additional income. However, success is not as simple as just putting out a "for rent" sign.

In this book, you'll discover the secrets behind being an Airbnb host. It's not just about renting a room; it's about creating a welcoming space for travelers. You'll learn about the myths and truths of being a host and the best practices for ensuring success through the journey to see if maybe one day, you could be a host too!

⭐ We Need Your Reviews!

Can you help us by reading this book and telling us what you think? Your reviews help other people understand what this book is all about and decide if they should read it.

📚 How to Share Your Thoughts:

1. Read "Airbnb for Beginners Made Easy".
2. Think about how Airbnb is different from renting a home for a long time and how it can be a profitable venture.
3. Click on the QR Code.
4. Write a few sentences about your favorite parts or what surprised you.
5. Send us your review!

Your thoughts are really important to us and to everyone who's curious about this world. Plus, sharing your review is a great way to help other people be successful on their journey.

Thank you for helping us out, and we're excited to see what you have to say!

Happy reading and exploring,

Qivist Publishing

FIVE

Set Yourself Apart

I t's time to set yourself up on the Airbnb platform! After all the research and reading, it's time we move on to the next step of the process which will involve your creating an account, listing your property, and learning some useful tips and strategies that will help you make your property stand out. Already feeling excited? Well, let's get to it.

Worrying About Your "Unique" and "Unusual" Properties

The eagerness and determination to set up your Airbnb profile and get earning will always be there; however, the concern develops when a potential host looks at the competition—which can be intimidating—and feels like their property is either too unusual, unique, or unattractive enough to get the attention it needs. This is a real struggle for most beginner hosts, and I'm here to tell you that if you have the property, permission, and resources for the business, then you should definitely go for it.

A few years ago, I had a close friend go out of their way to purchase a house when Airbnb had just launched and started making waves. Because my friend had made the mistake of buying a house before doing all the research, she later came to learn what she was up against, and like most hosts, this left her feeling rather concerned and discouraged about her journey ahead. Because the house was in a fairly remote location that was a few hours away from the main parts of the city, she thought it would accommodate travelers looking for some quiet time away from all the hustle and noise that comes with living in the city.

After buying the house and doing all the research to study the Airbnb requirements, understand the steps she would need to take to join the platform, and calculate how much revenue she could make, I guess seeing what she was up against left her feeling like she had no chance of making it in the business.

Many hosts who purchase "unusual" and "unique" properties often feel this way when they look at their immediate competition and see the numbers. However, I'm here to tell you that as unusual and unique as your home may be, the Airbnb platform is home to thousands of guests who are all searching for a unique experience. This unique experience could have them spot your listing and feel like, "This is the perfect home for me". But to spot your home, you would need to put in the work to get your property up, make your listing attractive, and ensure it's being found by the right target audience. Simply put, any property has the potential to become a great success. It all just depends on how you go about putting in the work behind the scenes. Today, my friend's property is doing incredibly well, and I like to use her story to inspire others to not look down on the opportunity but use competition as an inspiration rather than a threat.

How to Create Your Airbnb Account

By now, you should have answers to the following questions:

- Is hosting for me?
- Do I understand the legal aspects of this business?
- Do I have all my permits and paperwork in place?
- What are my thoughts on the business after exploring and analyzing my market?

When you've made up your mind to join the business, understood the legalities, completed the permits and paperwork, and conducted your market research, it's time you work on creating your Airbnb account to list your property, and you can start this by visiting www. airbnb.com. After loading the homepage, you can head over to the "Sign Up" icon which will lead you to the registration page. Signing up on the website can be done on your browser but you can also register on the platform through the Airbnb mobile app. Simply go to your app store, type "Airbnb" in the search bar, download the app, and install it. After opening the app, select the option to sign up on the platform. During the signup process, you'll be asked to provide your name, surname, email address, contact number, Google or Facebook account, and Apple ID. If you're living in South Korea, you'll need to include details on your Naver as well.

While registering on the platform, make sure you go through the site's terms and conditions. Airbnb may be large enough to provide hosts with numerous opportunities and support; however, there are host reliability standards that you should be aware of. These include standards and guidelines on listing accuracy, communication, and cleanliness. So, make sure you educate yourself on these to avoid consequences that could seriously cost you in the future.

One of the things I can truly commend Airbnb for is the straightforward process they've implemented to help hosts sign up on the platform. It's a free registration that will need only a few of your basic details. When it comes to documentation, all the platform will require is a submission of your government ID. That's it!

Knowing the Ground Rules

After creating your host account, it's time you studied Airbnb's ground rules. These rules apply to all hosts and are there to protect all parties while ensuring guests are guaranteed a safe, reliable, and comfortable stay when it comes to bookings, communication, listing accurate information, and ensuring your property is clean and well maintained at all times. Should you be found compromising these standards, this will reflect in your guest reviews as each guest will have the opportunity to share their experience.

Your Ground Rules

Let's look at the ground rules that apply to all guests.

Positive Review Ratings

With Airbnb, you must ensure you maintain a high rating on your overall reviews. Granted, you will encounter some difficult guests along the way, but in this case, patience is key because low ratings should be avoided at all costs. Fortunately, it doesn't take much to please the average guest because all you need is to focus on these four things:

- committing to all your reservations
- responding promptly to all communication
- providing accurate details on your listings
- ensuring your property is kept clean at all times

Reservation Commitment

As a host, you have a responsibility to honor every one of your reservations while ensuring you provide an easy and reliable check-in experience. This is done in two ways:

- **Not canceling confirmed reservations:** Unless there's a valid reason as to why you're canceling a reservation, you should avoid doing this at all costs. Certain unfortunate circumstances will be out of your control, but in such cases, you should alert your guest of this well in advance to allow them to make any necessary changes to their reservation and trip plans.

- **Providing guests with reliable access to the property:** Part of committing to every reservation means providing your guests with reliable access to the property when they check-in. This includes providing them with the right keycodes and directions to the listing.

Timely Communication

Co-hosts and hosts should make themselves readily available to respond to any unexpected issues or questions that guests may have before or during their stay. Prompt responses are ideal for all guest communication; however, this doesn't mean that the platform doesn't consider the everyday demands that hosts have to attend to in their personal lives. So, when we talk about timely communication, this will depend on the stage of the guest's trip, the nature of the inquiry, and the circumstances at hand. Let's look at appropriate, timely communication at these stages of your guest's trip:

- **Before the stay:** This stage of your guest's trip is five days or more before their stay. Here, you'll be expected to respond within three days of receiving any communication from your guest. Although the reservation will have been confirmed, most guests still reach out to find out some additional information as they prepare for their trip during the months or weeks leading up to their stay.
- **Leading up to check-in:** This stage of your guest's trip is on the day of check-in. Here, you need to prioritize responding to your guests as quickly as possible, which means within a one-hour time frame. If a guest reaches out to you, it's likely because there's an issue with their access, a missing key, or something along those lines. The one-hour window should be done during local daytime hours;

however, if you're unresponsive outside of the local daytime hours, the Airbnb team steps in to assist.

- **During the stay:** This stage of your guest's trip is anywhere between the first five days of their stay. During this time, it's best to respond to all guest communication within 12 hours of receiving a message during local daytime hours.

Listing Accuracy

When a guest reserves their booking, every detail on the listing should be accurate when it comes to describing the property's features and amenities from the moment they arrive to the moment they leave. Here's a look at what needs to be 100% accurate:

- **Booking details:** As a host, you're only allowed to change your booking details with prior consent from your guest if they've already made the reservation.
- **Location:** You have to make sure your location's information is correct when you list it. This includes all the details concerning points like your property's map pin and address. Something else you should include is any information concerning the property's surroundings, especially when it comes to noise.
- **Type, privacy, and size:** While listing your property, make sure you accurately describe the type of accommodation you're offering. So, is it an entire home or private room that you're letting out? Be clear on the listing's setup. How many bedrooms does the listing include? What are the sizes of the beds? Also, state the property's level of privacy. Are there other guests on the property? Is there an on-site property manager?

- **Property:** The description you provide and the photos you upload should match what the guest finds when they arrive. In other words, there needs to be an accurate representation of what the space is providing and if the listing needs to be substituted for whichever reason, you need to get approval from your guest first before making any changes to the booking.

- **Amenities, features, and house rules:** As a host, you need to disclose every one of your house rules. You also need to clarify which features and amenities are available to guests when they book the listing. So, does the property include a gym, hot tub, or kitchen? Again, these need to be accurately represented. Also, you need to be clear on any restrictions associated with using and accessing these amenities. For example, if the listing comes with a pool, make it known if the pool is only available during certain hours of the day or if it's closed during certain months of the year.

Listing Cleanliness

When it comes to the subject of cleanliness, your property needs to remain clean at all times and not pose any health hazards. This needs to stay this way before, during, and after your guest's stay.

- **Health and safety:** As mentioned, your space should always be free of health hazards. This includes issues with pests and mold.
- **Cleanliness:** Your listing should always meet Airbnb's strict standard of cleanliness. This standard will be high for some; however, advising hosts to list properties that are free of dirt, mess, extensive dust, and pet dander is only to

ensure your guests have the best experiences while staying on your property.

- **Guest turnover:** Every host needs to ensure they clean their property between each stay. This includes wiping surfaces, sweeping and vacuuming floors, doing laundry, and taking out the trash.

Host Violations

It's worth noting that with Airbnb, guests are advised to report violations as soon as they happen. Like the support the platform offers hosts to report guest violations, guests also have channels and guidelines to follow when they're dealing with an actual or suspected violation. This includes encouraging guests to:

- Communicate with hosts via the Airbnb messenger option.
- Document any issues that they may be having with the help of message threads sent to the host and photographs.
- Reach out to the Airbnb resolution center to report the matter and possibly request a refund.
- Leave an honest review on the host's listing to make the host aware of the guest's challenges.

Holding Hosts to Ground Rules

Airbnb may offer hosts numerous opportunities to turn their short-term rental businesses into a complete success; however, the platform is committed to ensuring all hosts adhere to its ground rules. Although the Airbnb platform consists of thousands of guests and hosts, it does open channels of communication when a problem has been reported. This means that each host is responsible for ensuring they follow the rules, and if this violation is to be reported, the platform will inform the host of its policies to ensure there's a clear understanding of what the ground rules are and depending on the problem at hand, some situations may call for a warning, suspension, or complete removal of your account.

With Airbnb, the platform looks out for both the host and the guest. This means that in the event of a violation, in addition to a warning, suspending, or removing your account, it can also take other actions that include refunding a guest their reservation or canceling an active or upcoming booking. This will all depend on the nature of the violation.

As a host, you're advised to avoid being responsible for a cancellation or canceling confirmed reservations, as this goes against the platform's Host Cancellation Policy. Should you be found doing this, you may face cancellation fees; however, if the reasoning behind your cancellation is valid and beyond your control, this may be excusable.

Appealing Violations

If you face a violation and feel you would like to appeal it, you can do so by contacting Airbnb's customer support team or using a link the platform provides to all hosts who would like to undergo the process of appealing a violation. As comforting as this process may sound, your efforts will be futile if you can't provide the platform with additional details to prove that the circumstances of the violation were otherwise.

List Your Property

Listing your property on Airbnb is a straightforward process. Here's how you'd go about it:

1. By now, you should have created and registered your account using your personal details. After signing up, you need to complete your profile by adding your profile picture, name, and brief introduction about yourself. Completing your profile is optional, but it comes highly recommended as it helps guests establish some form of trust with you.

2. After creating your account and completing your profile, you need to navigate your homepage until you find the "Airbnb your home" icon. You'll find this in the upper left corner of your page. When you click on this icon, each step will guide you through the process of listing your property on the platform. Each series of steps will be pretty

straightforward on what you should provide. Make sure you read the instructions carefully.

3. Now it's time to describe the space you're listing that will give potential guests a clear idea of what to expect. Use the steps to guide you on how you would go about describing your property, and make sure your description and title are detailed and compelling enough to highlight all your property's best amenities and features, but while doing this, remember to be accurate and honest so your guest's expectations match what's being sold to them. Remember to specify all the amenities your listing will offer. This includes things like WiFi, a kitchen facility, and a parking facility. After listing the amenities, discuss your house rules and cancellation policies.

4. After describing your space, it's time you upload images of your property. Make sure these are high-quality photos that showcase every aspect of your property. To attract potential guests, keep your photos well-lit and bright.

5. Set your nightly rates by considering factors like current market rates, facilities, and location. You can also use this time to set and add discounts to help you attract more potential guests. This will get you closer to getting your first booking and earning your first review.

6. After covering all the steps above, you need to take the time to review all the information you've provided to ensure everything is complete and accurate. From time to time, the platform may need you to verify your identity and you can do this by submitting some required documents. They can also ask that you register your short-term rental business with your local government, depending on your location, and all this may need to be done prior to your listing going live.

7. Once you've ticked all the Airbnb listing requirements, you can list your property on the platform by clicking "Publish listing." This will mean that your property has now been listed, and guests from around the globe can start viewing and considering your accommodation.

Optimize Your Listing

Let's look at how you can optimize your listing with the help of your listing's title, description, and photographs.

Title

Your listing's title is one of the first things your potential guests will notice and use to convince them to explore your property. For this reason, there are guidelines you should follow to help your title stand out and spark interest in the reader. Here are the top strategies that I've used over the years to create this interest:

- Keep your titles short by not exceeding a limit of 32 characters so it's easier to read when the site visitor is using a desktop or mobile device.
- You may consider using a title case or capitalizing all the words in your title to make it more attractive and convincing. However, in my experience, it's best to write your title in sentence case as this will make it more conversational and easier to read.
- Try using words as opposed to emojis and repeated special characters. Symbols and emojis often mean different things to people, and a good example of this is the thumbs-up symbol. For some, this symbol can be seen as a sign of approval, while for others, it can be an offensive gesture that means something completely different. To avoid any misleading or confusing details, make your title easier to read and more inviting by using words.
- If certain information has already been provided in the guest's search results, it isn't necessary to repeat it. Therefore, use your title to attract the attention you desire by adding unique details.

- Construct your title according to what you know your typical guest expects and needs. In this case, avoid composing a title that you hope will appeal to everyone. Instead, create a title that will appeal to your target audience, and you can do this by including suggestive words.

- You may need to find creative ways to save characters in your title, and if you find yourself in this position, consider using abbreviations. Good examples of this would include using "w/" for "with," "BR" for "bedroom," "BA" for "bathroom," "APT" for "apartment," "AC" for "air conditioning," "DT" for "downtown," and the like.

- Avoid using generic adjectives and words in your title and this includes words like "good," "nice," or "great." If you're looking for words that will best describe your property, rather choose something catchy, illustrative, and unique. Good examples of this would include words like luxury, couple's getaway, instaworthy, resort, eclectic, oasis, rare, hidden gem, green, contemporary, glamorous, peaceful, secluded, or peaceful.

- To make your title a little more captivating, include the listing's best features. This means highlighting the amenities that you know attract the most attention, like having a hot tub or swimming pool area or offering free WiFi and parking to guests. Including promotions and discounts would also be great. Finding your property's best features may be a little tricky to do in the beginning; however, with time, positive reviews can help you identify which features your guests love and appreciate the most.

- If you've made any upgrades to your property and believe this would add a competitive edge, consider mentioning this in your title to emphasize upgrades.

- Instead of mentioning your listing's neighborhood or city, try mentioning nearby landmarks that you know will likely make a traveler's time more convenient. This could be anything from shopping malls to tourist attractions.

Proven Title Formulas

Figuring out how to construct a catchy and unique title will be a little overwhelming at first; however, here are useful examples I've adopted over the years and these have proven to be a great success:

- Adjective, property type, "w/", and a top feature: An example of this would be, "Luxury Private Cottage w/ Double Bed + Ocean View."
- Adjective, property type, "near," and a landmark: An example of this would be, "Spacious 2 BR Near Local Museum."
- Adjective, property type, "perfect for," and an experience type: An example of this would be, "Modern Beach Apartment Perfect for Family Getaway."
- Enjoy, selling point, "at," adjective, property type, "in" or "at," and a location: An example of this would be, "Enjoy Ocean View at Fully Modern 3BR Condo in the Forest."

Description

After the title, your listing's description is the next thing your potential guests will look at. So, let's see how you can compose a description that's impressive enough to turn a potential guest into an actual customer.

Why Is Airbnb Listing Description Important?

You may spend a lot of time obsessing over composing the perfect title or getting the best photos for your profile but don't underestimate the power of a compelling description. With the right technique, you can easily turn a quick browsing experience into a confirmed booking when you know your audience and can highlight the points that make your listing stand out from the rest. Clarity and appeal can do wonders for you in this case, so let's see how you can put together a solid description that will increase the chances of your property getting booked.

Writing Tips for Describing Your Airbnb

Let's look at some tips on how to write your description for your Airbnb listing:

- **Target audience:** Before writing your description, know your target audience so you have a clear picture of who your ideal guests are. For example, are your ideal guests adventure seekers, couples who want a romantic getaway, families, or business travelers? When you know your ideal guest, you'll effortlessly compose your description in a way that will best suit your target audience. Always remember that it's your content and tone that will make listing more appealing to the type of guests you intend to attract.
- **Features and amenities:** Make sure you highlight any unique features and amenities as this will make it stand out from many of the other listings on the platform. So, whether there's a cozy fireplace, closeness to any popular tourist attractions, a modern kitchen, or a breathtaking view, try making this the highlight of your description.

- **Language:** Having a description isn't about putting together some convincing sentences. Your description needs to be just that—descriptive. Therefore, use descriptive language that will help paint a clear picture of what the potential guest can expect while staying on your property. Don't be afraid to evoke some emotions and imagery while doing this. For instance, instead of telling your reader that your property has a "large garden," consider saying something like, "spacious garden space that's perfect for a cup of tea or morning yoga session."

- **Clarity:** With descriptions, Airbnb only affords you 500 characters to sell your property, and trust me when I tell you that this is often not enough to get everything in. So, while it's important to be as descriptive as possible, you also need to prioritize clarity and conciseness because these are equally important. Sometimes, you may feel the need to sound overly professional but complex jargon and sentences only confuse potential guests. Rather, focus on being straightforward and clear about stating your case so all your readers have a clear picture and understanding of what you're trying to say.

- **Accuracy:** From time to time, you may feel the need to make your description compelling enough to attract guests; however, you must make sure every detail you provide is accurate. Whether it's about how far your property is from the city, the number of beds you have, or whether or not your kitchen is fully equipped, all details concerning your property need to be accurate. To avoid misunderstandings, you may consider keeping your descriptions as vague as possible but this isn't always a good idea because being vague can leave a lot of room for misinterpretation and this can spark a lot of negative reviews along the line.

- **First impressions:** Before uploading your description, make sure you check your information for spelling, typos, and grammar. These are an important part of accuracy and taking these for granted could create a bad first impression.
- **The bad and the ugly:** Let's say your property is in a noisy area or located on a busy street, this could be a potential downside that you may not want to address or mention upfront. Although it does make sense to put your best foot forward to compose a compelling description, it often works in your favor to be upfront about the bad and the ugly. Because downsides like these can be rather discouraging, consider framing the bad and the ugly, positively. For example, if your property is located on a noisy and busy street, mention this in a way that implies that the property is great for vibrant travelers who enjoy the nightlife and don't mind staying in the heart of the city with clubs and bars that are only a walking distance from their stay.
- **Keywords:** Keywords do a great job of making your listing more visible to your target audience. For example, if a traveler on business is viewing your listing, you'll want to include words like, "workstation" or "home office," if your property appeals to business travelers who are looking for space. Including such keywords in your description improves the platform's search results in connecting you to your guest. Furthermore, you may also want to consider including your property's neighborhood and city.
- **Expectations:** Your guests will have expectations from the moment they come into contact with you and it's your job to ensure you meet those expectations each time. In such a case, transparency and honesty are your best bet when it

114 • AIRBNB FOR BEGINNERS MADE EASY

comes to what your property does and doesn't offer. So, if your listing doesn't include parking or a fast internet connection, it's better to let them know. When you do this, you keep your guests informed and this prepares them for what's to come. This will improve their experience and guarantee positive reviews at the end of their time with you.

- **The other bits:** You may find certain parts of your Airbnb listing to be more important than others; however, everything including the images you upload, the list of amenities, neighborhood descriptions, and house rules play a part in influencing your potential guest's final decision. So, be as thorough, accurate, and detailed as possible in every section of your listing.

- **Leveraging:** You can always enhance how your listing appears by capitalizing on Airbnb's management software. This will help you tackle daily tasks associated with managing your property, helping you save time and resources on more effective ways to handle your business.

Photos

After your title and description, the next thing you need to focus on is your photos. These will work to showcase your rental and everything it offers. With that in mind, your photos can either make or break a person's decision to reserve their booking with you. So, let's look at how you can take those exemplary pictures, get the attraction you need, and maximize your bookings.

How Many Pictures Should I Upload?

With Airbnb, you can upload up to 100 pictures for a single listing. While this can be great news for many, realistically speaking, we all know that a potential guest will likely spend time going through the first 15 to 20 images before making up their mind. Therefore, there's no guarantee that uploading to the max will improve your listing. Instead, to make the most of this opportunity, choose up to 10 high-quality pictures that are bright and clear enough to help your visitor have a proper idea of what you're offering.

In reality, having 10 high-quality pictures is far better than having 50 poor-quality pictures that are grainy and blurry. However, discouraging you from uploading too many images doesn't mean you should have too few pictures because this may not give potential guests enough of a clear picture of what you're offering and this could come off as suspicious. So, make sure you're balanced in all avenues.

Are There Any Requirements for My Airbnb Uploads?

With Airbnb, the only requirements it has for photographs uploaded on the platform are the following:

- Photos need to have a resolution of at least 1024 x 683 px.
- 3:2 is the width-to-length ratio you need to apply to your photos.

Fortunately, the platform doesn't have any strict regulations for hosts uploading images on their profiles but they do offer guides on how to go about sizing and styling your photos so they appeal to guests in the best way possible.

Is There Any Equipment That You Would Recommend?

We live in a time where smartphones are just as effective as digital and professional cameras; therefore, you can always adjust your smartphone or camera to suit the goals you have in mind. In this case, you may want to invest in a tripod to balance your camera so photos come out crisp and clear.

How to Take the Best Photos for Your Airbnb Listing

If you have the budget to hire a professional photographer for your photos, then you're more than welcome to do so. However, if you're a beginner who's on a budget and ready to learn a thing or two, here are eight helpful steps that you can use to get the best shots for your listing:

1. **Clean and declutter:** Clean and declutter your rental so it's spotless by the time you're ready to shoot. Messy, cluttered, and unclean spaces often put potential guests off; therefore, to make your space appealing, consider arranging your furniture, washing and packing dirty dishes, removing visible stains, mopping or vacuuming your floors, packing away clutter, and organizing any ornaments or books that may clutter the space. Then, make sure you prepare each room, open all your blinds and curtains, organize your coffee table if you have one, thoroughly clean the bathroom, and make sure the countertops in your kitchen are sparking.

2. **Turn on the lights:** When your rental is clean and free of clutter, you need to focus on your visual display and this means incorporating excellent lighting in your photoshoot as it makes your images look more professional. First, you'll want to start by opening all the blinds and curtains in your rental. This will allow all the natural sunlight to enter each space. When that's done, you can look at finding the right light source. You may think of capitalizing on artificial lighting in this case; however, try natural light first as it often enhances your rental's colors, depth, and

contrast. After this, consider turning all the indoor lights as this will eliminate dark corners that could show up in your photos. Especially with bathrooms and kitchens that don't have as much natural light, turning on the indoor lights will afford your potential guests a clearer view of what your rental offers.

3. **Shooting into corners:** We often shoot while facing a wall directly; however, to get more dimension to your picture's composition, consider shooting into a corner. In addition to giving your potential guests a better perspective of how space is in each room, it also makes spaces appear more inviting and bigger. What I love about shooting into corners is that you can use this technique in all rooms, including the shower and kitchen space of your rental. Then, when it comes to focal points, the bed, sofa, bath or shower, and stove or oven would be the focal points for the bedroom, living room, bathroom, and kitchen, respectively.

4. **Focus on the details:** Hosts often make the mistake of only wanting to capture all the major amenities overlooking the smaller things, not knowing that these can also make or break a potential guest's final decision. For example, think about outdoor sheds or a vegetable garden that your property may have. These *insignificant* features can add to your guest's experience. So, before you think of dismissing these, remember that it's the small things that add character to your home.

5. **Taking panoramic shots:** When you want to showcase an entire room in just a single shot, consider taking panoramic shots. These are pictures that show a field of view that's greater than or approximating what the natural human eye would see, thanks to the use of lenses that come with wide angles, giving potential guests a better idea of how big

your space is. Shots like these often credit everything you detail in your description and when it comes to outdoor spaces, consider using vertical shots.

6. **Use different angles:** Avoid using the same angle when you're taking pictures because this will eventually come off as slightly underwhelming. For variety, use different angles to capture your best shots but make sure you don't leave out any amenities because you can easily get caught up in wanting to appear artistic.

7. **Paint the ideal lifestyle:** Potential guests appreciate practicality in images; however, many of them choose rentals based on the lifestyle they offer. Use your collection to showcase this. For example, if your property has a rustic feel to it, include the cheeseboard and copper stovetop kettle or if it has a sleek feel to it, include the luxury items you've added in each room. With pictures showcasing the kind of lifestyle you're offering, this will attract your ideal target market

8. **Showcase the town:** If possible, try capturing images of the neighborhood your rental is in. Potential guests often love this and as you do this, make sure you stick to capturing the feel and essence of your neighborhood. In this case, one or two images are enough.

Making the Most of Your Airbnb Photo Section

Now that you have all the perfect shots, let's see how you would go about enhancing your listing's photo section on Airbnb:

- To organize your images, categorize them according to the area and room they're in.

- Don't be afraid to upload your best shots and most attractive photos first.
- Provide a caption to each of your images.

DIY or Hire a Photographer: Which Is Best?

With basics on how to take the best images for your listing, you need to sit down with yourself and think about whether the guidelines provided above are enough to help you get the pictures you need. Remember that everything mentioned in this chapter will either make or break a potential guest's decision to go with you; therefore, working with a professional photographer may work if you have zero photography experience. In this case, their skills, experience, and specialties can help you get exactly what you need for your listing. So although this will come at a cost, it may be worthwhile in the end because you also need to factor in the high-tech equipment and editing software that you'll need to help polish and sharpen your photos.

House Rules

Guests will often find house rules to be limiting and *boring* at times; however, as a host, you impose these to set expectations on how you want your rental to be treated. Granted, the more *flexible* your rental seems, the more appealing it will be to potential guests; however, if you intend to protect your property and its amenities from damage and don't wish to inconvenience neighbors, this may be the best possible solution to your problems and concerns.

House rules exist to help you manage your rental business more efficiently and each time your guests comply with them, this helps you avoid future problems that could require your or Airbnb's intervention. Furthermore, when guests understand these rules, it reduces the likelihood of you receiving negative ratings and reviews. Other benefits of including house rules include the following:

- All parties are fully aware of your expectations.
- You can better maintain your property's safety and security.
- House rules centered around cleanliness can help prevent damage.
- You reduce the likelihood of spending time and energy dealing with conflicts, complaints, and misunderstandings.
- You're able to create a more positive experience for you and your guests.

How to Compose Your Airbnb House Rules

When you list your house rules, these should be centered around the following:

- cleanliness
- litter
- damage
- approved guests
- check-in time
- checkout time
- smoking
- pets
- noise
- commercial filming and photography

Depending on your preferences and concerns, you'll list your house rules accordingly. Here, balance is key though because too many house rules may scare potential guests away while too few house rules may cause problems for you soon. Therefore, it may be a good idea to stick to common rules like the following:

- No smoking inside the property. If a guest needs to smoke, this should be done outside and only in a designated area.
- No events or parties are allowed as the hours between 10 PM and 7 AM are regarded as quiet hours.
- Guests need to keep the property clean and tidy at all times. If the property is left excessively dirty, the guest will be charged a cleaning fee.
- Without prior approval, guests aren't allowed to bring additional guests as an additional fee may apply.
- Guests should keep their noise levels down out of respect for neighbors.
- When guests temporarily leave the property or checkout, all appliances and lights should be turned off.
- Guests should immediately report any issues or damages to the property.
- Guests should avoid eating and drinking on beds and the couch.

How to Establish Effective Airbnb House Rules on the Platform

Establishing effective house rules doesn't require any kind of rocket science. Here are nine guidelines that I've used over the years:

- keep your rules simple and precise
- be specific
- identify safety concerns and address them immediately
- make sure your standards and requirements are attainable
- keep your attitude friendly and firm
- use positive language

- make sure your communication is straightforward and clear
- send your guests a copy of the rules
- update your rules regularly

Instructions on How to Add House Rules to Your Listing

Each time a potential guest or guest visits your listing, they will be able to view your house rules the moment they access the listing. Also, while concluding their reservation, they will need to agree to your house rules through an acknowledgment that the platform implements. So, to add house rules to your listing, you'll follow these simple steps:

1. On the page, click on "Listings."
2. Select the listing you wish to add your house rules to.
3. Go to "Policies and Rules."
4. Go to "House Rules."
5. Add or adjust your house rules.
6. Click "Save."

The Airbnb Commitment

When it comes to the platform's commitment to house rules, Airbnb plays its part by providing information about the various issues, warnings, and policies each guest should be aware of. When a guest is found to be repeating these violations and ground rules, the platform will suspend or remove their account altogether, making it every guest's responsibility to ensure they're aware of all the policies and warnings that each host stipulates.

Earlier in the section, I provided you with a list of common house rules that most hosts list. These are regarded as standard house rules and if you happen to have additional rules that you would like to add, you can include these, and all your guests will be notified of them in advance. Should the guest violate these rules, the platform will rule in favor of the host and support them if the host feels the reservation needs to be canceled.

Reporting Violations to Airbnb

As a host, Airbnb will always encourage you to report violations as soon as they occur. You and neighbors can report these violations directly to the platform but if a neighbor reports a violation to you or suspect one is happening, you have the option to

- reach out to the guest to resolve the matter.
- use pictures from your observations or neighbor's report to post this on the platform's message thread.
- leave feedback for the guest to use in the future.
- report the issue directly to Airbnb.

Booking Policies

Airbnb has a cancellation policy that includes a set of guidelines on ways to promote clarity and fairness for hosts and guests. These guidelines notify hosts and guests of what happens when a reservation is canceled and depending on the circumstances at hand, different rules will apply.

The Four Types of Cancellation Policies

When a reservation undergoes cancellation, depending on the circumstances, the platform will place it under one of four policies that will determine when the guest can cancel the reservation, how much their refund will be, and how far in advance they would need to cancel this reservation to be eligible for this refund.

Let's look at the four Airbnb cancellation options:

- **Flexible policy:** As the policy's name suggests, this is Airbnb's most laid-back and flexible option for guests. Here, your guest will receive a full refund if they cancel no less than 24 hours before check-in, and should they cancel within this 24-hour window, you'll get to keep the full reservation payment while qualifying for an extra night's booking. The advantage of this policy is that the platform's algorithm often favors listings with this policy and this will increase the chances of you getting more bookings. However, the disadvantage of this policy is that you, as the host, aren't protected from cancellations. So, if your guest is to cancel one week before check-in, you lose this revenue together with other bookings that you could have accepted during this time.

- **Moderate policy:** Although Airbnb favors the flexible policy, hosts typically opt for the moderate policy because of the balance it offers for guests and hosts when it comes to flexibility and protection. The advantage of this policy is that hosts aren't victims of last-minute cancellations since guests have until five days before check-in to receive a full refund. Should they cancel anytime during this five-day window, you'll get to keep the payment while enjoying an extra night's pay and half of the unused nights.

- **Strict policy:** As the name suggests, this policy is pretty much strict and the greatest disadvantage of this policy is it offers less flexibility but on the flip side, it protects hosts 100% of the way. Under this policy, guests can get a full refund if they cancel within 48 hours of them securing the booking. They can also get a full refund if they cancel 14 days before check-in. If the guest cancels at least one week before check-in, they will be eligible for only 50% of their payment. This refund will include the cleaning fee and not the service fee. If it's any time less than the one-week window, the guest won't be eligible for a refund.

- **Long-term policy:** This policy applies to reservations longer than 28 days as the rules here are a little different from the shorter stays. If a guest cancels their reservation, they need to do so at least 30 days before check-in to be eligible for a full refund and it's worth noting that they won't get their fee back for the first month. Should they choose to leave early, they will need to pay for 30 days after the day of cancellation or until the amount they would have paid if they'd stayed the entire stay. The advantage of this policy is that if a guest cancels less than 30 days before check-in, you will have a full month's reservation to look forward to and this can be a great financial cushion. However, the disadvantage of this policy is that accepting such reservations would mean lowering your rates to stay competitive. You also need to consider the possible wear and tear that will come with housing people for long periods of time. This could spark issues along the way. While reservations like this would be great when you're looking to get a steady income, it does come with its fair share of ups and downs.

Airbnb Extenuating Circumstances Policy: What Does This Mean for the Cancellation Policy

Ever since the COVID-19 pandemic, Airbnb has gradually been adopting the Extenuating Circumstances policy and this policy guides all parties on how to handle unforeseen events that are beyond the host or guest's control when they arise after the reservation has been made and it's now challenging to commit to the booking.

It would do you some good to go through this policy in detail to see how Airbnb protects all parties in this regard; however, when it comes to what this policy excludes, this includes:

- flight cancellations
- flight delays
- seasonal weather conditions that were expected and reported
- sudden injury
- sudden personal illness
- delayed or rescheduled personal appointments and engagements

Then, when it comes to policy inclusions, this is what it includes:

- natural disasters like tsunamis and earthquakes
- pandemics, epidemics, and emergencies that have been declared by the government
- prohibitions or travel restrictions that the government has imposed
- conflicts involving various hostilities
- conflicts that involve armed forces

Airbnb Cancellation Policies That Apply to Hosts

Airbnb is committed to providing pleasant experiences for all guests and one of the things it aims to minimize is cancellations initiated by hosts. For this reason, the platform has a policy that aims to address host cancellations but, of course, it will make provisions for hosts canceling for reasons beyond their control. Unfortunately, there is a fee you will be charged for canceling a booking but this will depend on the number of times you've canceled a reservation before and the situation at hand. So, here are some things you need to be aware of:

- The platform will deduct a certain fee from your next payout if you've canceled over seven days before check-in.
- If you cancel a booking less than seven days before your guest's arrival, you will be charged a different fee for that. This fee will be higher than the fee you would have paid if you had canceled at least seven days before check-in.
- You won't be charged a cancellation fee if you've had at least consecutive bookings that you haven't canceled yet.
- The platform will block a certain number of days on your calendar when you cancel a reservation.
- Airbnb will notify all parties if you happen to cancel a reservation. In this case, guests will be allowed to leave a review on your listing; however, the platform will allow you to explain your side of the story in such a case.

If you can prove that you're unable to host your guest due to extenuating circumstances, Airbnb may approve your cancellation without any penalty. Examples of this include:

- the government unexpectedly changed travel requirements
- natural disasters
- pandemics, epidemics, and emergencies that have been reported by the government
- unauthorized events or parties
- governing agencies limiting or prohibiting travel to your listing's location or from it

- hostilities
- military action

Always remember to cancel booked reservations well in advance, if possible, to allow guests to adjust their plans accordingly. If the booking needs to be done within 24 hours of check-in time, you won't be able to do this online and will need to contact Airbnb directly.

When Guests Are Eligible for a Refund

There are additional refund policies and cancellations that you should also be aware of when it comes to guests and possible refunds that you would possibly issue if your guest checks in but find the following:

- The accommodation cannot be accessed.
- Information on the listing wasn't accurate.
- The guest felt that their health and safety were at risk.

In Conclusion

Airbnb's cancellation policies all aim to provide a balanced approach to addressing various concerns and needs made by hosts and guests. So, depending on your concerns and needs, you will choose a policy that will suit your situation as each policy will provide you and your guest with the fairness and clarity you need to handle a cancellation. Remember that choosing the right policy will play a crucial role in how best you'll maximize your bookings, especially when it comes to the experiences you'll be offering your guests. Therefore, as a host, learn these policies in and out, and understand that the platform has been designed to foster reliability and trust on the platform because both guests and hosts wish to have a fruitful and rewarding experience.

SIX

Determining Your Price

N ow that you've set up your listing, it's time you work on determining the rates you'll be charging. Unfortunately, with a rental business, there's a lot you need to consider when finding the right price for your listings and you also need to have knowledge of

Airbnb's fees to make the most of your revenue and not spend a lot of your earnings paying for one expense and the next. So, let's look at how you would go about determining your price.

Understanding Airbnb Fees

Like the fees that guests incur for a reservation, Airbnb also has fees that apply to hosts for using its platform to list and rent out their property. These fees apply to all bookings and before your income is paid out to you, the platform will subtract its fee from your earnings. For now, this may sound pretty straightforward; however, as you unpack this a little more, you'll see that different host fees depend on your fee structure and the kind of booking you're offering.

What Percentage Does Airbnb Take?

Hosts are subject to a standard service fee of 3% of the total booking amount. But before you have your sigh of relief and think, "That's not bad," you should know that the platform offers hosts different fee structures that you can choose from, depending on what best suits you. Numerous factors influence your fee equation but in addition to this fee structure, you should also factor the cancellation policy you'll be applying to your bookings. So, if you've chosen your fee structure and applied a strict cancellation policy to your listing, your fee can go about 2% higher than what you'd be charged if you'd chosen a flexible policy. This makes it incredibly important to learn and understand Airbnb fees; otherwise, your business may not be as profitable as you expect.

It's free to list your property on Airbnb and this is regardless of how you'll choose to craft your listing when it comes to its title, description, the number of images you'll upload, and the rates you'll set. The only time you'll start incurring fees is when you start accepting bookings.

Understanding Airbnb Service Fees

As an Airbnb host, you will be subject to service fees and these are calculated as a percentage of how much your guest will pay to reserve their booking. This reservation fee will include the possible additional fees such as cleaning fees and nightly rate. To get a good idea of this, you can expect to be charged anywhere between 5% and 15% of the guest's total reservation (Clark, 2023).

When it comes to service fees, these will differ from host to host but with Airbnb, these are categorized into two fee structures so let's look into these to understand them better.

Split Fees

Most hosts opt for the split fee and that's because hosts get to share this fee between them and the guest. For most hosts, this fee will be about 3% of the reservation's total but there are exceptions that you should be aware of. For example, if you're a host listing in Italy and have chosen the Super Strict cancellation policy, this will increase your split fee a little more than what the average host would pay if they were in a different part of the world. To calculate this fee, Airbnb will factor everything that goes into the reservation's subtotal and this includes the nightly rate and guest fee that will apply to a guest adding someone else to the reservation. This fee doesn't include tax and when you're ready to receive your payout, the platform will automatically deduct this fee from you (Clark, 2023).

When it comes to how Airbnb would go about charging guests with a split fee structure, usually, this fee amounts to about 14.2% of your guest's reservation total. To calculate this fee, certain factors will be considered like any additional guests that your guest will be inviting, cleaning fees, and the nightly rate. This percentage will vary, depending on numerous factors but everything will be included in the total amount the guest will pay during the checkout process. If your guest will be staying for a period longer than three months, the platform will charge less when it comes to the guest's service fee and this will help the guest save some money on their end (Clark, 2023).

Host-Only Fees

This fee structure is a lot more straightforward because you're in charge of settling all Airbnb fees in full instead of having your guests cover part of the fee. The fee is usually a little higher than what you'd find with your split fee but this is typically anywhere between 14% to 16%. It's important to note, however, that factors like how long your guest will be visiting and which cancellation policy you've chosen will influence this fee. And like the split fees, choosing the Super Strict cancellation policy will only increase the fee and those staying longer will get to enjoy some reduced rates. The fee structure you choose will depend on you but if your listing is into traditional hospitality, you must choose this fee structure.

When it comes to Airbnb fees for hosts using iCal or a channel manager, like hosts in traditional hospitality, it's mandatory to use this fee structure if you're a software-connected host. This is known as Simplified Pricing and you're charged 15% of your guest's total reservation fee. You'll have the option to choose between Split-fee or Host-only if your listings are based in the following locations (Clark, 2023):

- U.S
- Uruguay
- Canada
- Taiwan
- the Bahamas
- Argentina
- Mexico

How to Check Your Reservation's Service Charges

As a host, you'll be responsible for settling host service fees, VAT, and other taxes that will come with every booking that's made on your listing. Fortunately, this won't include fees like cleaning costs, extra guest fees, security deposits, and cancellation fees as these are charges that your guest will be responsible for. This is great news for all Airbnb hosts but as you calculate rates, you must make sure you add these guest fees to your listing so all Airbnb fees are covered with each booking.

With everything we've discussed so far, it's time you start setting your rates and this can be a little tricky to do at the beginning. However, as you work on finding the perfect balance, here are some additional costs you should be aware of and include as you work on concluding your rates.

Cleaning Costs

This is a fee you will include in your rate to cover the expense of cleaning your space after your guest checks out. Adding this fee to your booking price is optional but should you choose to not include a cleaning cost in your price, you will need to have alternative ways of paying for a cleaning service.

Co-Host Payments

A co-host is a friend, family member, or other individual that you can work with to help you manage your listing and guests. On Airbnb, you have the option to share your reservations with your chosen co-host if you happen to have one. Depending on your agreement, you will work out a way to split profits in a fixed amount or percentage of each reservation.

Cancellation Fees

Life can sometimes get in the way of things but platforms like Airbnb continue to establish cancellation policies to avoid disruptions in the event of something unexpected happening. We've already talked about how hosts are affected and compensated for cancellations that guests have initiated but should you choose to cancel a confirmed booking, there is a cancellation that you will need to settle. Airbnb aims to minimize distractions at all costs; therefore, imposing charges on cancellations will help minimize the chances of it happening.

When you cancel a confirmed reservation, the fee you'll need to pay will depend on when the cancellation has been done and this means the following (Clark, 2023):

- If your cancellation occurs less than two days before check-in, you'll be charged 50% of the reservation amount for the nights remaining.
- If your cancellation occurs after check-in, you'll be charged 50% of the reservation amount for the nights remaining.

- If your cancellation occurs between 2 to 30 days before check-in, you'll be charged 25% of the reservation amount for the nights remaining.
- If your cancellation occurs more than 30 days before check-in, you'll be charged 10% of the reservation amount for the nights remaining.

With this reservation amount for the nights remaining, it's worth noting that this includes pet fees, the cleaning fee, and the base rate. It doesn't include guest fees or taxes and for Airbnb to get its charges, this owning amount will be withdrawn from future payments to you to guarantee that the fee is paid. It's only under exceptional circumstances that a cancellation fee may not apply.

Other Costs

In addition to the fees mentioned throughout this chapter, there are some additional costs that you or your guest may need to also pay, depending on factors like location, currency conversions, and the bank you and your guest are using. In this case, it would be a good idea to contact your bank for assistance and guidance on any questions that you may have regarding these fees.

How Do I Avoid Paying Service Fees on Airbnb?

As a business owner, it's only natural to want to collect as much of your profits as you can, and learning about the Airbnb service fees can be slightly disheartening. Unfortunately, it's nearly impossible to bypass your host fees when you list on Airbnb; however, there are alternatives you can explore the platform's different fee structures to keep your booking channels diverse. For example, many of the short-term rental business owners I've come across have created their own vacation rental websites. With the experience that they gain from Airbnb, creating and launching their own websites has allowed them to accept direct bookings while bypassing the various service fees that we've discussed so far from platforms like Airbnb.

Nowadays, the internet makes it possible for us to connect with different resources that make it possible to learn virtually anything, even as a beginner. Several platforms allow business owners like yourself to create direct booking websites that are simple, stylish, and beginner-friendly enough to help you achieve your goals. All of this is possible without any technical experience. If you already have a website that you're using for direct bookings, you can simply link the booking widget to reserve bookings in just a few steps. It's that simple!

Strategies to Manage Fees

Where profits are concerned, the thought of the various expenses and charges you'll be incurring can tempt you into setting some pretty high rates; however, considering the competition, balance will be key. So, here are five strategies you can use to navigate these difficulties and eventually find that sweet spot.

Building Fees and Costs

You can always use insights and analytics to weigh your costs against Airbnb fees. Using these tools will help you avoid losing money in the long run because everything will be measurable. As previously advised, you should be fully aware of the costs that will come with running your short-term rental business before setting your rates. This means investigating expenses like Airbnb fees, maintenance costs, and cleaning fees. When you know these costs, you'll be able to set rates that will cover your costs while leaving enough room for profits.

So, let's say you initially thought of charging $100 for your listing. If your costs amount to $15 for each booking, you may want to add this fee to your initial rate and adjust it to something like $115 to leave enough room for profits while keeping the rate competitive.

Stay Competitive

Each time you set your rates, you need to remember to stay competitive; otherwise, you risk having no business at all. As an Airbnb host, you're up against non-hotel listings that are also on the platform and hotels. To make sure you're operating on an even playing field, find out what other hosts are charging in your area and then measure that against your rates and what you're willing to offer because having more to offer will allow you to charge more for your listing.

If you find that your listing isn't any different from what other listings in your area are offering, consider adjusting your prices to match the competition or you may struggle to find business. If you wish to keep your rate and find that it's slightly higher than your competition, consider finding ways to make your listing more valuable. In the beginning, this will be easier said than done, but with time, you'll get a hang of it.

Switch Things Up

Thankfully, Airbnb charges are fixed and don't change according to factors like seasonality. However, adjusting your rates according to demand and supply will be necessary to help you maximize profits. When the demand for short-term rentals is low, it may be a good idea to drop your rates to secure a booking during slow months. Then, when the demand picks up, you can increase your rates to take advantage of the busy months.

Make the Most of Add-Ons

Your Airbnb fees are made up of your nightly rates and any additional fees that you'll charge your guests for things like adding an extra guest and cleaning. To increase profits, consider maximizing add-ons that you can charge. For instance, some listings offer guests an airport pickup service, guided tours, breakfast meals, and more. These add-ons will make your listing more valuable while allowing you to charge fees that Airbnb won't have a share in.

Don't Rely on Airbnb Alone

Airbnb isn't the only platform or option you have to establish your rental business. If possible, try listing your property on other platforms as well. This will help you maximize bookings and with a website of your own, you're able to cut out the middleman and get the most of your profits.

Repairs vs. Maintenance of a Rental Property

When we talk about property maintenance, we're talking about the operation, oversight, maintenance, and control of physical property and real estate. This includes:

- Land real estate
- Commercial properties
- Residential properties

You have the option to maintain your property yourself but you can also hire a property manager or property management team to take responsibility for all the day-to-day maintenance, upkeep, security, and repairs for your property.

Rental Property Maintenance Expenses

Vacation homes have maintenance expenses that usually concern the following:

- lawn care
- plumbing
- replacing damaged appliances
- electrical repairs
- roof repairs
- pest control
- flooring
- painting

In addition to the list above, you also need to pay hazard insurance to protect your property from damage that natural events like an earthquake, fire, tornado, or severe storm could cause. As a beginner, it will be a bit of a challenge for you to know exactly how much money you would need to allocate to maintain your property, but thankfully, there are different approaches that you can explore to figure out how much you would need to spend on property maintenance annually. As unique as each approach will be, the numbers and overall goal will remain the same so you'll pick an approach that you know will best suit the type of rental property you own. What's important is to make sure you have enough money to fund unexpected emergencies and your routine maintenance checks.

With a vacation rental property, you have three approaches that you can use to figure out how much you'll need to spend on maintenance costs annually (smartbnb, 2022):

- **The 1% rule:** This approach requires you to put aside 1% of the value of your property each year. You'll use this money to settle expenses related to maintaining your rental. So, let's say your rental property is worth $250,000. The 1% rule says that you'll set aside $2,500 for maintenance.
- **The 50% rule:** This approach requires you to put aside 50% of your monthly rental income for insurance, repairs, taxes, and maintenance. This will help you cover all your property costs.
- **The square footage rule:** This rule will have you cover your annual maintenance costs by requiring you to set aside $1 for every square foot of your property. So, let's say your property is 2,000 square feet. To maintain your property, you'll set aside $2,000 each year.

The budget you allocate to maintaining your rental property will also depend on whether you're doing all the maintenance yourself or outsourcing a team. While doing it yourself will cut down on the expense of needing to hire a team, it's important to do an honest assessment of your availability and skills before making that final decision. Choosing either option will come with some considerable pros and cons but one of the main advantages that I've always admired about hiring a team is that you can use your time to focus on more important aspects of your business.

A Property Maintenance Checklist: Why You Need It

Maintaining your property regularly is crucial when you're in the business of short-term rentals and there are main reasons for this but today, I'd like to focus on two reasons. First, there's a lot you can prevent through routine maintenance, especially with the big things. Some issues can grow and develop into something huge in the long run that will often require an emergency repair which is usually costly and a hassle to get through for any property owner. Routine maintenance will help you prevent such emergencies from happening and this will keep your property, its features, and appliances in good condition. This will help reduce your maintenance costs.

Secondly, every guest wishes to have a pleasant experience when they're being hosted. When you keep your property clean, safe, and functional, this keeps your space in good working condition. It also indicates a great deal of responsibility on your part which later translates to 5-star reviews. It's important to note that although it's up to you to choose how far you're willing to go to maintain your property, by law, every rental property needs to maintain strict safety and health standards. This includes ensuring that your major systems are also functioning the way they should. To maintain these standards on your part, you need to conduct property inspections as often as you can; otherwise, issues concerning your property will only arise when your guests bring them to your attention. In this case, a rental inspection checklist would help you identify minor issues so they don't turn into major emergency problems. The checklist will also help you remember every essential part of your inspection process to help you not forget anything important.

Airbnb Maintenance: What Are Host's Responsibilities?

Turning your Airbnb venture into a successful business will require a great deal of hard work, patience, and proper maintenance. So, in my years as an Airbnb host, I've developed a checklist that I believe will help many beginners who are keen on knowing what the important tasks should be while encompassing the hard work, patience, and proper maintenance that your business and property will need:

Task	Yes	No
Do a pest inspection monthly or quarterly to ensure your property is free of pests		
Test and replace the batteries in your carbon monoxide and smoke detectors		
To prevent mold, check your property for leaks and water damage		
To prevent deterioration, check your bath, shower, and sink for caulking		
Every six months, check your service cooling and heating systems		
Every three months, replace the air conditioning systems and duct filters		
Every six months, inspect your water heater by flushing it		
Check your property's gutters and roof		
Make sure the locks to your windows and doors are secure		
Check your property's common areas for any safety risks that could cause harm		
Prune all the shrubs and trees on and around your property		

Make sure your property is clean before and after every reservation		

As you grow in the business of short-term rentals, you'll gradually add to this checklist and personalize it so it suits you. Furthermore, experience will help you create maintenance schedules for larger projects that will include tasks like replacing carpets and repainting the walls. When your property is well maintained, this provides your guests with better experiences while reducing the chances of you needing to attend to emergency maintenance requests. Then, should you experience an emergency maintenance request, make sure you take action immediately. An immediate response will show your guests that you care about their experience and this will likely keep your overall rating at a high score.

Having a guest raise an issue regarding your property's maintenance will put you in a bit of a panic when you're concerned about the rating they will give you. Routine maintenance will help you avoid emergency maintenance requests but this won't guarantee that they won't happen. So, should it happen, remain calm and be as responsive as possible by answering all your guest's questions as quickly as you can while sending help to get the problem fixed. Fortunately, Airbnb has a messaging system that makes it easy for you to connect with guests anytime they need you. Of course, you won't be available to attend to requests 24/7 but you can put measures in place to be responsive and attend to any guest matters.

Do Property Managers Pay for Repairs?

The simple answer to this is that hosts are responsible for settling their routine maintenance costs, even if they have a property manager who has been outsourced to help the host manage their maintenance tasks. Airbnb will protect its hosts by using a form of payment to replace or repair items that a guest has damaged; but the host will still be responsible for routine maintenance costs in line with changing air filters, fixing your everyday wear-and-tear, and replacing the batteries to your fire alarms.

Tips to Handle Rental Property Maintenance

When it comes to how you can go about handling maintenance for your rental property, there are three options that you can try to ensure your property stays in excellent condition all year round:

- You can handle your property repairs and maintenance yourself. This will require a great deal of handiness and time on your part but you'll be saving yourself a lot of money by choosing to perform these maintenance tasks yourself.
- You can outsource a property management company to handle certain tasks. How much you'll be spending on the service and what type of tasks they'll be handling will depend on your contractual agreement but outsourcing such a service will be of great help to you in the long run.
- You also have the option to maintain your property yourself but outsource local professionals who will get down to all the *dirty* work. For instance, if your guest happens to report an issue related to your plumbing, this problem can be directed to you; however, you can hire a local plumber to get the problem fixed. Over time, you'll establish relationships with these local professionals and develop a team of people who will help you maintain your property anytime you need them.

In Conclusion

Setting your nightly rates doesn't mean waking up one morning, finding what your competitors are charging for their listings, and proceeding to charge the same. A lot goes into determining your price and before you jump in excitement for the profit potential you may be looking at, consider the costs and fees that you'll need to tackle to stay in the business of renting out your property.

Unfortunately, short-term rental fees and costs are an inevitable part of your business venture; therefore, do all you can to avoid certain fees like cancellation fees, be sure to settle Airbnb for its host fees, and maintain your property regularly to avoid paying the huge price that will come with facing an emergency. So once your price has been set, it's time you learn about how you can become a superhost and that's coming up in the next chapter.

SEVEN

Become a Superhost

When guests are searching the Airbnb app and looking for accommodation, they will sometimes come across listings with the title *Superhost*. Simply put, this means that the host of that particular listing has met a series of Airbnb requirements that rank them as being highly responsive, consistent in achieving high ratings, unlikely to cancel a reservation, and often booked.

When a potential guest understands this, it only improves your chances of getting booked so I've dedicated this chapter to showing you what it means to be a superhost, how you can achieve and maintain this title, and the different ways you can navigate and overcome common challenges that make it difficult to reach this status or maintain it.

What Is an Airbnb Superhost?

When you join the Airbnb platform as a host, you'll find that there are types of hosts—regular hosts and superhosts. Everything we've discussed so far is in line with being a regular Airbnb host but when you reach the status of being a superhost, this means that the platform has recognized you as being one of the hosts who continue to go above and beyond to fulfill your duties and provide your guests with an exceptional experience. In honor of your service, Airbnb will reward you with a red and orange badge and this badge will appear on your profile anytime a potential guest comes across your listing. This will add a layer of credibility and trust to you and your listing.

What many hosts appreciate about the superhost program is that any host can reach this status, whether you're offering simple private rooms or running several luxury properties. The program is essentially about rewarding a host's service and has nothing to do with luxury, exclusivity, or uniqueness. This offers all hosts the amazing opportunity to "get their flowers" and be honored by the platform on a public scale.

Why Did Airbnb Launch the Superhost Program?

As mentioned before, Airbnb launched the superhost program to reward and celebrate hosts who go above and beyond to consistently offer exceptional service to any guest who is under their care. As a beginner starting in the business, for some time, you will be regarded as a regular host who provides an average service to guests. However, with time, you can work your way up to being recognized as a superhost. This will differentiate you from other hosts, making it known to other hosts and guests that you're an excellent service provider.

Airbnb uses a standardized and comprehensive system of metrics to find its superhosts and this becomes an additional markup to what hosts already have on their profile ratings. Moreover, in addition to the requirements we'll be discussing a little later in the chapter, the platform also considers your portfolio as a whole in the manner in which you've been managing your property or properties.

How to Become an Airbnb Superhost?

Airbnb has a set of criteria that it uses to determine who can become a superhost, and when you meet these criteria, the platform will notify you of this new development and award you with the badge. This means that there's no way for you to necessarily apply for the status. All you need to do is ensure that you're delivering on the set metrics that Airbnb has established.

So, you may be wondering how this works. Well, every three months, the platform will evaluate your performance as a host in the last 12 months but if you haven't been on the platform for longer than 12 months and are doing exceptionally well as a host, you can also be eligible for the status. For five days, Airbnb will assess your performance and this will take place on the first of January, April, July, and October. Should you meet Airbnb's stipulated requirements on any of these assessment dates, you will be notified of your achievement and receive your badge within a week of the assessment period.

It's worth noting that earning the superhost status doesn't mean that the title will remain on your profile indefinitely. After earning the badge, you'll be tasked with maintaining your credibility and exceptional service. If you do not meet the criteria during any of the quarterly assessments, you will immediately lose your status and have the badge removed from your profile. It's worth noting that even though you're assessed every three months, your metrics are established on how you've been performing in the last 12 months.

Therefore, to maintain your status and reputation, make sure you're always monitoring your cancellation rates, response times, and overall ratings. Where possible, avoid making unnecessary mistakes that could affect your guests' experiences, and make sure you meet the key requirements to maintain an impressive performance.

The Benefits of Becoming an Airbnb Superhost

Some hosts stumble upon the privilege of being rewarded with a superhost status while others strive to achieve it. Either way, becoming a superhost is optional and by gaining such recognition, to guests, other hosts, and Airbnb, being a superhost isn't just about having a colorful badge grace your profile. Numerous advantages come with this level of status, including exclusive rewards and higher earning potential.

More Bookings

Potential guests are always looking for the best experience so unless they've been hosted by a specific host before, there's no real way of knowing which host will provide them with an exceptional or average service. Being a superhost tells potential guests that you're reliable and this makes your listing stand out while reassuring potential guests that you're ready to provide them with the best experience there is. According to research, it's said that hosts often get an increased occupancy rate of 81% when they earn the title of being a superhost. Therefore, this isn't something to take lightly.

More Visibility

When your listing earns the superhost badge, it stands a greater chance of being featured on the platform's curated lists and newsletters. Also, many people who visit the app searching for accommodation and are looking for reliable hosts often narrow their options down to superhosts only, and this is thanks to the platform's search filter that allows this. When this happens, you gain visibility and according to research, superhosts see a 5% improvement in the amount of traffic their listing receives when they rank among the superhosts.

It Inspires Trust

Becoming a superhost tells potential guests looking at your listing that you don't cancel bookings and are willing to offer an outstanding experience. This inspires trust and is very reassuring to guests.

An Increase in Your Average Daily Rate (ADR)

Guests know that you'll be providing them with a premium experience and service; therefore, as a superhost, you can increase your

ADR and not necessarily have to worry about the competition you'd be facing if you were a regular host.

An Increase in Income

When trust, an increasing ADR, a high occupancy rate, and visibility are on your side, this will automatically grow your income. According to research, earning this status has increased the income of most superhosts by up to 60%.

More Recognition Among Your Network

Becoming a superhost isn't something you should take lightly because guests and fellow hosts on the platform develop a great deal of respect for you when you achieve such a status. Considering how challenging the business can be, having the honor of being a superhost helps you gain the recognition you deserve and as you grow in the business, you'll gradually build a network that will have you enjoy some beneficial privileges among other hosts.

Enjoying Exclusive Rewards

If a superhost happens to maintain their status for a full 12 months, they receive a $100 travel coupon. In addition to this, there's a referral program that they can take full advantage of where superhosts get to earn an additional 20% on their existing referral bonus each time they successfully manage to register a new host on the platform. There are also local Airbnb events that they get to attend and a feature that you'll get in Airbnb's official newsletter.

Ongoing Dedicated Support

Airbnb does its best to offer customer support to all hosts in the best way possible but this can sometimes be a frustrating experience for many regular hosts. As a superhost, you get to enjoy dedicated support from the platform because you receive priority treatment that will allow you to offer your guests a better experience, resolve matters sooner, and enjoy a better overall experience with Airbnb.

A Superhost's Earning Potential

According to research, between October 2021 and September 2022, it's said that superhosts generated a collective income of more than $23 billion from hosting their properties on Airbnb (Airbnb, 2023a). Also, let's not forget that the average superhost makes 60% more revenue than a regular Airbnb host. There's more to being a super-host than just acquiring a badge for your profile and it's all centered around there being tangible evidence to prove that you're hard-working, committed, and dedicated to providing your guests with the best experiences while fully investing in your journey as an Airbnb host. Granted, you'll get the chance to enjoy more bookings and charge more with your rates but this ranking is mainly about the high-quality experience you continuously deliver to your guests.

Airbnb's Requirements for Becoming a Superhost

Should you eventually earn the title of a superhost, always remember that the pressure is now on to maintain this title because this isn't an indefinite position to hold. Like every other host on the platform, Airbnb will still do its quarterly assessment of your profile and in the event of you being unable to meet their require-ments, you will lose your badge. Essentially, Airbnb's requirements are set out as follows (smartbnb, 2020):

- Your overall rating as a host needs to be at an average of at least 4.8 stars or more.
- You need to have hosted at least 10 stays in the last 12 months.

- Your cancellation rate must be lower than 1%.
- You need to have a response rate of more than 90% for all your guest messages and this needs to be within a window of 24 hours.

It's worth noting that should you have more than one listing, you need to achieve the set metrics on all your listings. But let's look at these requirements in greater detail to know exactly what's expected of you.

Reservations

Your first requirement is to complete a minimum of 100 nights or 10 stays for at least 3 trips. This is to assess your ability to maintain an exceptional experience in hosting.

Response Rates

The next requirement is to maintain a response rate of at least 90%. Part of providing potential guests and guests with good service involves responding to their messages as quickly as possible. To be a superhost, Airbnb expects you to maintain a response rating of no less than 90% and it's important to note that this will require a great deal of effort and time on your part, as it will likely take you away from attending to other hosting duties. For this reason, you're advised to consider automating your messaging to balance your hosting duties.

Cancellation Rates

To earn the badge of becoming a superhost, you need to maintain a cancellation rate of no more than 1%. Simply put, this means that for every 100 reservations that you get, you're only allowed to cancel 1 if you're looking to become a superhost. Of course, there are exceptions to this but that only applies to incidents that fall under the platform's Extenuating Circumstances Policy, which we discussed earlier in the book.

As a host, you may consider listing your property on other platforms or you may be managing more than one property. Managing several properties is one thing but listing your property on more than one platform means that you're likely to get overbooked sometimes and this is the common reason most hosts end up canceling reservations on Airbnb. To avoid this, consider connecting your calendars with the help of a property management system. The internet offers hosts in the property game numerous options and you can find one that will best suit your budget, ideal features, and overall preferences.

Overall Ratings

Lastly, to become a superhost, you need to earn or maintain an overall rating of at least 4.8 stars. This will be based on guest reviews and the platform considers ratings in the last 12 months. To ensure your guests leave positive feedback and reviews, you need to ensure you provide them with excellent service throughout their time with you. To generate a steady flow of positive reviews, you can always opt for automated guest messaging and guest review templates that will help make this possible.

What Is the Airbnb Response Rate and Time?

Hosts often take responsiveness lightly because many typically respond to the questions and concerns guests present when they're able to but if you're striving to become a superhost, your response rate and time will influence your eligibility greatly. Successful hosts respond to messages from their guests as soon as they come in and as challenging as this may be, some resort to putting measures in place to ensure their guests are attended to at every given moment. Furthermore, it's worth noting that hosts who typically respond on time usually rank higher on the Airbnb platform in guest searches.

When it comes to communicating with your guests, you may be a lot more involved and dedicated to responding promptly after your guests have arrived to ensure everything is going smoothly with their stay. However, you should exercise the same dedication and effort before the reservation has been concluded and in the days leading up to check-in because that's the time your guests will need the most information about the reservation. The same applies to the day they check out. They may have some important questions to ask as they prepare to leave your property. For this reason, prompt responses are needed throughout your time with a guest because different questions and concerns could arise at any given moment. So, let's understand the difference between response rates and response times to know how Airbnb calculates the overall response rate that gets used to determine eligibility.

Understanding the Response Rate

Airbnb calculates your response rate by taking your listing's reservation requests and new inquiries and looking at how many of them you responded to by either declining, pre-approving, or accepting them within the space of 24 hours for 30 days. So, let's say a potential guest reaches out to you via Contact Host and sends an inquiry or asks a question, although this isn't a reservation request, you would still need to respond to the potential guest within a space of 24 hours to keep your response rate looking good. If, for instance, the potential guest decides to have you host them, they will send you a reservation request and you will have 24 hours to either accept or decline the request to keep your response rate looking good. To determine whether or not you qualify to be a superhost, the platform will assess your response rate over 365 days.

Understanding the Response Time

Airbnb calculates your response time by looking at the average amount of time it takes you to respond to every new message that arrives on your listing. For regular hosts, the platform will monitor this response time over 30 days but to determine whether or not you qualify to be a superhost, the platform will assess your response time over 365 days.

Points Worth Noting About Response Rates and Times

When you're starting your rental business on Airbnb, based on everything we've discussed so far about marketing, competition, and searches, depending on your techniques to get noticed, it may take some time for your listing to get noticed and booked. As a result, some hosts tend to panic about their response rate and time out of concern that they may not have enough communication coming in to determine a response rate and time for your profile.

The good news is that even as a beginner, this can be calculated. For guests who receive less than 10 new messages in the space of 30 days, the platform will use those few messages to calculate your response rate and response time within the last 90 days.

When it comes to calculating your response rate, remember that this is a percentage amount that will represent the number of new messages you respond to within 24 hours for 30 days. It's worth noting that your response rate doesn't only apply to reservation requests that you can choose to accept, pre-approve, or decline. It also applies to new inquiries from guests. If you take more than 24 hours to respond to new inquiries and reservation requests, this will increase your profile's average response time and decrease your response rate.

How Can You Improve Your Response Rate and Time on Airbnb?

Fortunately, it doesn't take rocket science to improve your response rate and time on Airbnb. Essentially, everything is about checking in with your host account as often as you can and responding promptly if something has been communicated to you. But let's see how you can improve your response rate and time a little further.

To improve your response rate and response time, you need to do the following:

- With reservation requests, you need to accept or decline these within 24 hours of receiving them.
- With trip requests, you need to pre-approve or decline these within 24 hours of receiving them.
- With new inquiries from guests, you need to respond to these within 24 hours of receiving communication.

If you respond to any of these requests or new inquiries after 24 hours, this will count as a late response. Responding to these new messages will increase your response time; however, because your response will come only after the 24-hour window, this will decrease your response rate, impacting your position on the platform's search results. Moreover, follow-up messages won't affect your response rate. This means that you don't have to be the last one to send a message to your guest to maintain your response rate.

Host Cancellation Policy

To become a superhost, the golden rule regarding cancellations is that you need to maintain a cancellation rate of less than 1%. This does come with an exception if the reason for cancellation falls under the Extenuating Circumstances policy but let's look at this a little further so you have a better understanding of how this works.

Cancellation Fees

Hosts rarely initiate a cancellation and if it does happen, this is usually due to circumstances that are beyond their control. Cancellations can be a massive inconvenience for guests who have already reserved a booking with you because it often disrupts their plans and indirectly undermines their confidence in the platform. For this reason, when a host cancels a reservation that's already been booked, this pushes Airbnb to impose a cancellation fee and some additional consequences to the situation at hand.

Hosts need to understand that cancellations often affect guests, Airbnb, and the host community at large in one way or the other; therefore, you should only cancel a reservation if it's for a valid reason and if the cancellation is happening under extenuating circumstances, the platform can offer an exception. You can refer back to Chapter 6 on how Airbnb goes about calculating its cancellation fees when a host cancels a reservation.

Exceptions to the Rule

As mentioned in the previous chapter, certain situations may waive a cancellation fee if you happen to experience an event that falls under the Extenuating Circumstances policy or have a valid reason as to why you're unable to host your guest. Should you believe you're part of the exception, you will need to provide Airbnb with documentation and other support to prove that your cancellation is valid and true. After looking at the evidence you present to them, that's when Airbnb will decide on whether the cancellation and additional consequences can be waived.

Consequences You Should Be Aware of

Unfortunately, avoiding the cancellation fee won't guarantee being excused from facing additional consequences. For instance, the platform may choose to block your listing's calendar to prevent you from securing another booking during the affected dates. Again, this will depend on the circumstances at hand but something worth noting is that regardless of Airbnb's final decision, you still won't receive a payout for your canceled reservation.

When You're Found Responsible for a Cancellation

Should you not have a valid reason for canceling a confirmed reservation, you could face some serious consequences in line with the platform's terms and conditions, and ground rules. For example, some hosts have their accounts or listings suspended while others lose their title as a superhost or have their accounts removed altogether. In that light, be careful to not do the following because you will be found responsible for a cancellation if your reasons are in line with any of the following:

- Listing a property that's later found to differ from what the guest finds when they arrive
- Double-booking your listing
- Replacing your listing with a property that's different from what the guest had booked
- Listing inaccuracies that later disrupt a guest's stay like saying that your property offers a pool when it doesn't

What Else to Consider

In the event of you needing to cancel a reservation, make sure you do so well in advance to allow your guest enough time to make those necessary changes. Regardless of the circumstances at hand, taking the steps to cancel a reservation will require you to take full responsibility for this change, and even though the consequences ahead won't be ideal, advising your guest to initiate the cancellation on their end is something you should avoid at all costs.

While you undergo the process of providing Airbnb with the proof and documentation they need to confirm your reasons for canceling your reservation, make sure your materials and statements are true because providing inaccurate and untrue information does violate the platform's terms of service. So, should it be found that you've provided false materials and statements, you may face some serious consequences that include a termination of your account.

Maintaining an Overall Rating of 4.8 Stars

As a host, you'll do all you can to construct a listing that's compelling enough to have any potential guest decide to be hosted by you. Because all you have to sell your listing is mainly a title, description, and some photographs, guests are aware that you'll do everything it takes to make sure you're "the chosen one." Since marketing and advertising are all about putting out the good, reviews are an honest reflection of a guest's experience with you and your listing. Therefore, reviews and ratings are often a critical aspect of your profile because they can either make or break it.

When your listing is mostly made up of positive reviews, this builds an immediate sense of trust between you and your potential guest, even if they've never interacted with you before. Also, potential guests use ratings and reviews as a guide to make informed decisions and know exactly what to expect when they step into an agreement with you. With Airbnb, the platform aims to offer guests and hosts a fair review system that protects and respects all parties in its community. Therefore, as a host, it's important to do your best.

Deciding to join the Airbnb community will come with a great deal of excitement and zeal to put your best foot forward and make the most of this opportunity; however, one or two negative reviews can throw you off and leave you discouraged. Not all your guests will be the easiest of people to work and engage with and getting some unreasonable ratings can be an inevitable experience for many hosts. While it's important to not take such feedback to heart, a few negative reviews can also shed some light on a few things you could improve as a host. This allows for continuous improvement.

With guests, you never know what to expect but when it comes to effective ways to encourage them to leave Airbnb reviews, you can do this by:

- Asking guests to leave a review on the day they leave the property instead of reminding them to do so before check-in or during their stay as many tend to forget.

- Providing some detailed guidelines on how they can leave a review on your listing to make the process easier and convenient for those who may struggle to navigate the app.
- Sharing a message of thanks and appreciation to all guests who leave reviews on your listing.
- Showcasing and responding to both positive and negative reviews.
- Cultivating a culture of allowing your guests to leave honest reviews on your listing.

As you strive to become a superhost, your overall rating needs to be no less than 4.8 stars. Every review that gets left on your listing will count toward your overall rating but as a host, you can also leave a review on your guest's profile. Surprisingly, leaving reviews on your guest's profiles increases your chances of obtaining the Superhost status but this can be a tricky task to do when you're faced with needing to provide feedback on a somewhat difficult guest. Providing feedback on your easy-going guests will be effortless but doing so for difficult guests will require a bit of wisdom on your part because the last thing you want to do is share a bit of your mind on a public platform. So, to give out the best guest reviews for both positive and negative experiences, here are ways you can go about doing it:

- Avoid being hasty about leaving a review, especially when it has to do with an unpleasant experience.
- Remain positive and polite at all times.
- Get straight to the point.
- Provide constructive feedback that will help your guest do better in the future.
- Where possible, use templates to help save you the time and effort of needing to think of what to say.

- Should a guest respond to your review, be sure to respond.
- Remember to not reveal any personal information when writing a review.
- If possible, try to focus on the positive.

In some cases, you'll want to "agree to disagree" with difficult guests because going back and forth with them on why you're right and they're wrong will turn into a never-ending battle. In the event of there being a complaint or negative review about your service, remember that communication is key and do all you can to:

- respond promptly
- remain courteous and professional
- show that you understand your guest's concerns and grievances
- apologize when a certain event is your fault
- reassure the guest that you'll do better in the future

The Airbnb Review Process: How Guests and Hosts Can Leave Reviews

Both hosts and guests have 14 days to leave a review after check-out. Unfortunately, the only way you can see your guest's review is by submitting a review yourself or waiting for the 14 days to end. The same applies to your guests being able to see your review. When your guest checks out, you and your guest will receive an email from Airbnb asking you to leave a review and a link will be included in the email to lead you to the "Reviews" page so you can share your experiences. Should you not find a link in the email or have trouble accessing or using the link, there's an option to write the review on the app directly.

The Benefits of Leaving Reviews

There's a lot to gain from guests leaving reviews but some of the key benefits that I've appreciated over the years include the following:

- **Accuracy:** Potential guests have an opportunity to read through accurate responses attesting to your service delivery.
- **Value for money:** Positive reviews assure potential guests that being under your care will definitely be worth it.
- **Trust:** Real experiences from guests who have already done business with you will establish a foundation of trust between you and guests who are considering your services.
- **Promise:** Potential guests are assured of exceptional service if they choose to reserve their booking with you.

Maintaining Your Airbnb Superhost Status

As you grow in the business of being an Airbnb host, there are common challenges that you should be aware of and prepared to face. These include the following:

- having your guest change their check-in and check-out times
- having your guest cancel their reservation at the last minute
- facing amenity issues
- addressing concerns about noise
- hosting partygoers
- having your guest suddenly dislike you for no apparent reason
- having your valuables sustain damages

- having domestic items on your property get misplaced or stolen
- needing to address a negative guest review
- dealing with defective amenities
- constantly needing to communicate with guests
- facing emergencies
- dealing with difficult guests

When you finally earn the title of a superhost, the hard work doesn't end there because everything will now revolve around maintaining this status. In this case, Airbnb's standards and requirements will remain the same but what's important on your part is to make sure that you remain consistent in the quality of your service delivery. Additionally, other tips you should keep in mind include:

- prioritizing communication
- delivering high-quality experiences
- minimizing cancellations

In Conclusion

Becoming a superhost comes with many benefits that ultimately boost your income and get you the recognition you need to rank in some pretty high places. This makes it every host's goal. Granted, spending an entire year working hard to achieve this goal does seem like you'll be faced with a long journey ahead but Airbnb's requirements and standards make it possible for every host to earn their badge as it's relatively simple to get here when you add a great deal of consistency and communication to your role.

As with all agreements, educate yourself on Airbnb's policies, rules, and terms to know what's acceptable and inappropriate for hosts. This will help you avoid silly mistakes that could hinder you from earning your badge sooner rather than later.

EIGHT

Take It to the Next Level

W e've reached the final leg of our race and it's time we talk about the different ways you can streamline Airbnb's systems, take full advantage of their opportunities, and ultimately increase your bookings and revenue. Today's technology makes it possible for companies like Airbnb to improve their business models while technological innovation allows us as hosts to list our properties with ease so that guests can locate us and reserve bookings effortlessly.

As we break this chapter down bit by bit, I need you to remember everything we've discussed so far about optimizing your listings, calculating the right nightly rates, responding on time, and ensuring that you're constantly in communication with guests, the impact reviews have on your profile, remembering to limit the number of bookings you cancel, and ways to navigate and overcome common challenges that hosts across the globe typically face.

A recap like this can easily overwhelm you into thinking that the business of short-term rentals is pretty demanding and challenging, especially because each task is just as important as the next. By neglecting any of these points, you risk compromising the overall quality of your service and this can present some disappointing setbacks when you're aiming to become a superhost. This is the reality of being an Airbnb host and for you to manage your responsibilities in the most efficient and effective ways, you need to put systems in place to make sure that nothing gets forgotten and left behind.

In this chapter, you'll get to understand why Airbnb is a leading company in the hospitality industry and how it continues to influence competitors with its straightforward concept that offers effective strategies, tools, and technology to those who choose to make use of the platform. At the end of the day, being the best host isn't about being a superwoman or superman who can do it all. In this line of business, the secret lies in learning to work smart and this means finding creative ways to get the job done quickly and easily. So, let's look at how Airbnb makes that happen.

The Airbnb Instant Book

Of the many tools Airbnb has implemented to create smooth communication and booking processes for guests and hosts, the one that happens to stand out for me the most is the Airbnb Instant Book. This tool allows guests to make bookings in a few simple steps, helping them avoid needing to send hosts a reservation request first to receive approval. In this case, guests would need to own a fully registered account with the platform to make use of the tool but once their account has been set up, they'll have access to Instant Book listings at no additional cost to them. Many will benefit from this tool but it will be most convenient for guests who are trying to make those last-minute reservations.

As a host, using Instant Book means you won't have to review and accept reservation requests individually, and by making your listing available on the tool, you're likely to generate an even greater income. Other benefits include increased visibility, a booking process that's more streamlined, higher conversion rates, and the chance to foster greater trust and credibility between guests and hosts. To use the tool successfully, you would need to update your calendar as regularly as possible because not doing so could result in some unexpected bookings that could force you to resort to cancellation, and considering everything we've discussed so far about cancellations and fees, this is the last thing you want to do as a host. Therefore, to avoid any scheduling errors, always sync your Airbnb calendar with your main calendar.

Four of the main advantages that come with using Instant Book are that it's convenient, free, increases the chances of your property getting booked, and offers you peace of mind. However, some downsides should be noted and this includes mentioning that the tool

- doesn't accommodate hosts who have reservations that go longer than 30 days.
- isn't suitable for hosts who have unique personal requirements.
- doesn't cater to hosts who offer spaces that come with special challenges or features.

How to Make Instant Book Work Better for You

One of the best ways to make the most of Airbnb's Instant Book is to capitalize on its customization settings and tailored strategies. Here, you'll be able to

- create clear guest criteria that will help clarify prerequisites for all guests.
- implement precise cancellation policies to protect you from last-minute cancellations.

- request security deposits to discourage guests from damaging your property
- have guests sign rental agreements that will discourage inappropriate activity and behavior while providing you with legal protection from illegal or damaging activities.
- keep the lines of communication between you and your guest open.
- provide guests with a detailed and thorough welcome guide that explains all the expectations and rules you've set out for their stay.
- integrate your property management software with the Airbnb Instant Book to better manage your listing.

How to Turn Instant Book On or Off

Should you consider using Instant Book, you can activate the feature by logging into your Airbnb host account, choosing the listing you would like to enable the feature for, and opting to switch it on. Depending on your preferences, you can customize the feature to best suit you. For instance, some hosts customize the feature to only accept guests with verified identification or positive reviews. You can further customize it according to minimum stay, pre-booking message, and maximum guests. If you would like to deactivate the feature, you'll follow the same steps and choose to turn it off. It's just that simple!

Airbnb Instant Book Cancellation

As a host, you have the option to cancel a reservation without facing any penalty. There are a few reasons as to why you may consider this, like:

- The guest has some concerning reviews
- You've asked the guest some questions and they aren't responding
- The guest is implying that they will likely not comply with one or more of your rules and expectations

To cancel the reservation, you can simply log in to your host account, navigate to your list of reservations, select the reservation you would like to cancel, and choose "Cancel" to begin the cancellation process. The platform will ask you to provide a reason for your cancellation and you'll choose the reason that explains your decision.

Why Invest in Professionals?

Depending on your skills, budget, and availability, you may choose to outsource professional services to assist you with things like cleaning, lawn care, or bookkeeping. Hosts often have busy lives to manage; therefore, it can sometimes be a little challenging to do everything on your own, regardless of how much money you could save from hiring a professional.

Of the many things you can do yourself, one of the services I would advise every host to hire is vacation rental cleaners. Part of being an exceptional host involves providing your guests with a clean and comfortable space. With vacation rental cleaners, advantages you can look forward to include:

- improved guest satisfaction rates
- more time to attend to other important tasks
- the chance to showcase your attention to detail

- a chance to create and maintain a hygienic and clean environment for your guests
- consistent compliance with safety regulations

Hiring a professional cleaning service will increase your expenses; however, looking at the benefits above, there's more to gain from improving your guest's experiences, affording you the chance to attend to other things, and complying with health and safety requirements. But as you work on finding a suitable Airbnb cleaning service, questions you should ask and research include:

- Is it reliable?
- In the event of there being some last-minute changes, how easy is it to communicate these changes to the company?
- Is the company scalable?
- Can the cleaning service form a partnership with me?
- What do other Airbnb hosts have to say about the cleaning service?

Using Social Media to Promote Your Listing

From competitive rates and optimizing Airbnb search engine optimization (SEO) to guest reviews and listing yourself on various tourist websites, there are many ways you can promote your listing. Of the many ways you can do this, I often advise beginners to explore social media marketing and this is for several reasons which include the chance to do the following:

- grow awareness about your listing
- drive more traffic to your website
- enhance guest engagement
- gain guest feedback

- enhance your listing's visibility
- build your business brand
- network with guests and other hosts in the business

Contrary to what many believe, social media marketing is not difficult to learn or understand. You can also do it at no cost, depending on how big your following and audience is. If you have a large following, you have an audience that's big enough to get the word across through likes, comments, and shares. But if you have a small following, you have the option to make use of social media marketing tools that will allow you to advertise your listing for a fee and even if you're on a tight budget, you can find really pleasant packages to work with.

In Conclusion

You don't need a million dollars in the bank to take your rental business to the next level. By capitalizing on Airbnb's features, hiring a team of professionals, and finding creative, effective, and affordable ways to market your listing, you'll be well on growing your business in no time.

How to Share Your Thoughts:

Just A Reminder; We Need Your Reviews!

Can you help us by reading this book and telling us what you think? Your reviews help other people understand what this book is all about and decide if they should read it.

How to Share Your Thoughts:

1. Read "Airbnb for Beginners Made Easy".
2. Think about how Airbnb is different from renting a home for a long time and how it can be a profitable venture.
3. Click on the QR Code.
4. Write a few sentences about your favorite parts or what surprised you.
5. Send us your review!

Your thoughts are really important to us and to everyone who's curious about this world. Plus, sharing your review is a great way to help other people be successful on their journey.

Thank you for helping us out, and we're excited to see what you have to say!

https://amzn.to/4c3DuPI

Happy reading and exploring,

Qivist Publishing

Conclusion

We've come to the end of our journey together but I'm confident that this is only a start to your fruitful journey ahead. So far, we've talked about understanding what Airbnb is as a company, how to qualify yourself in the business, and which legal aspects you should be aware of. We also explored why it's important to examine your market, set yourself apart from every other Airbnb host, consider factors to determine your price, strive to become a super host, and do all you can to take your business venture to the next level. We've really come a long way!

Delving into every dynamic that goes into running a successful rental business can be overwhelming for some but by breaking every aspect of this venture down for you bit by bit, my goal is to educate you on everything you should be aware of to get you started. This will help you develop the confidence you need to step into this knowing exactly what you're doing. The lessons I've shared with you are based on research and experiences that I've encountered along my journey. Therefore, I can only hope that this will push you in the direction of starting your Airbnb venture and turning it into a complete success. Moreover, I've structured the book to follow the QUEST Method and by following this way of starting your journey, you'll navigate every avenue of this venture and not miss a single step of the process. Here, you won't go wrong.

Being an Airbnb host is not a walk in the park. It comes with common(and even uncommon)challenges you can find in the hospitality industry. But you don't have to figure it all out alone. With this book beside you, you will always have access to insider tips and proven strategies to help you navigate and overcome challenges to experience the satisfaction of being an Airbnb host sooner rather than later.

So, if you feel like this book has provided the headstart you need, please share your thoughts and experience in the form of a review to help others also find the help and guidance they need. Wishing you all the best with your journey ahead!

References

Airbnb. (2023a, February 15). *Airbnb celebrates 1 million Superhosts*. Airbnb Newsroom. https://news.airbnb.com/airbnb-celebrates-1-million-superhosts/

Airbnb. (2023a, March 9). *Why it's so important to respond quickly to guests - Resource Center*. Airbnb. https://www.airbnb.co.za/resources/hosting-homes/a/why-its-so-important-to-respond-quickly-to-guests-374?locale=en&_set_bev_on_new_domain=1711223861_YzVjNWMxZmVlMTFh

Airbnb. (2023b, October 23). *Guidelines for writing your listing title - Resource Center*. Airbnb. https://www.airbnb.co.za/resources/hosting-homes/a/guidelines-for-writing-your-listing-title-533?locale=en&_set_bev_on_new_domain=1711223861_YzVjNWMxZmVlMTFh

Airbnb cancellation policies | The ultimate guide. (n.d.-a). Hostaway. https://www.hostaway.com/blog/airbnb-cancellation-policies/

Airbnb cancellation policies | The ultimate guide. (n.d.-b). Hostaway. https://www.hostaway.com/blog/airbnb-cancellation-policies/

Airbnb house rules - actionable tips and examples. (n.d.). Hostaway. https://www.hostaway.com/blog/airbnb-house-rules-actionable-tips-and-examples/

Airbnb listing description: examples and guide. (n.d.). Hostaway. https://www.hostaway.com/blog/airbnb-listing-description-examples-and-guide/

Airbnb Meaning. (2023, June 20). IGMS. https://www.igms.com/airbnb-meaning/

Airbnb rules: 9-step checklist to stay within the law | iGMS. (2024, January 30). IGMS. https://www.igms.com/airbnb-rules/#

Airbnb titles: Proven formulas that attract 5x more bookings. (2020, April 27). IGMS. https://www.igms.com/airbnb-titles/

Airbnb vs. renting: Which strategy generates the best ROI? (2022, September 30). IGMS. https://www.igms.com/airbnb-vs-renting/#

Allen, J. (2019, June 4). *Do your homework before Airbnb-ing your property | Real Estate | Blog*. Bigger Pockets. https://www.biggerpockets.com/blog/short-term-rental-market-research

Andreevska, D. (2024, January 21). *Evolve rental property management review: What property owners need to know*. Learn Real Estate Investing | Mashvisor Real Estate Blog. https://www.mashvisor.com/blog/evolve-rental-property-management/amp/

BabyHandsAtArms. (2016a, September 26). *How my Airbnb hosting experience went (or how I learned to stop worrying and love the guest.)*. Reddit. https://

www.reddit.com/r/AirBnB/comments/54na24/how_my_airbnb_hosting_experi
ence_went_or_how_i/

Brown, L. (2023, June 9). *Advantages and disadvantages of Airbnb*. Linkedin.
https://www.linkedin.com/pulse/advantages-disadvantages-airbnb-lex-brown/

Carroll, J. (2023, August 8). *111+ quotes about homeownership you'll love*. Real
Estate Spice. https://realestatespice.com/quotes-about-homeownership/

Chen, J. (2022, May 31). *Unicorn Definition*. Investopedia. https://www.investope
dia.com/terms/u/unicorn.asp

Clark, R. (2023, October 26). *Airbnb host fees: How much does Airbnb take?* Vacation Rental Owners & Property Managers Blog - Lodgify. https://www.lodgify.
com/blog/airbnb-host-fees/

Clifford, R. (2020, July 3). *Airbnb tools: The complete list (2021 Update)*. Airbnb
Smart. https://airbnbsmart.com/airbnb-tools/#tve-jump-17128e70648

Colcol, S. (2023, June 5). *How to use Airbnb Instant Book for hosts*. Little Hotelier.
https://www.littlehotelier.com/blog/get-more-bookings/airbnb-instant-book/

Common misconceptions about Airbnb - Hometime. (n.d.). Home Time. https://www.
hometime.io/blog/common-misconceptions-about-airbnb

Debunking 14 common Airbnb myths: Insights from a super host. (n.d.). Jam and Tea
- Learn How to Live Life Better. https://www.jamandtea.com/start-airbnb-busi
ness/airbnb-myths-misconceptions

Debunking Airbnb myths | Top 10 Airbnb hosting misconceptions. (n.d.). Hostaway.
https://www.hostaway.com/blog/airbnb-hosting-misconceptions

Elphick, D. (2022, October 10). *Airbnb Superhost: How to become a Superhost on
Airbnb*. Little Hotelier. https://www.littlehotelier.com/blog/get-more-bookings/
airbnb-superhost/

Ground rules for hosts - Airbnb Help Center. (n.d.). Airbnb. https://www.airbnb.co.
za/help/article/2895?locale=en&_set_bev_ohttps://www.lodgify.com/blog/
airbnb-host-fees/n_new_domain=1711223861_YzVjNWMxZmVlMTFh

Host damage protection - Airbnb help center. (n.d.). Airbnb. https://www.airbnb.co.
za/help/article/279#:~

How to become an Airbnb host - Requirements. (n.d.). Lodgify. https://www.lodgify.
com/guides/airbnb/host/

How to take great Airbnb photos: An essential guide for success. (2020, November
24). IGMS. https://www.igms.com/airbnb-photos/

IGMS. (2023, March 23). *How the Airbnb business model works*. IGMS. https://
www.igms.com/airbnb-business-model/

Karani, A. (2019, August 7). *The 4 steps of Airbnb market research*. Investment
property tips | Mashvisor Real Estate Blog. https://www.mashvisor.com/blog/
steps-airbnb-market-research/

Karina. (2023, March 22). *Twelve Airbnb challenges hosts face - Opportunities and solutions*. Complete Hospitality Management. https://completehospitalitymanage ment.com/airbnb-host-challenges/

Nestrs. (2019, December 26). *Five steps to researching your Airbnb's market and regulations*. Nestrs. https://nestrs.com/5-steps-to-researching-your-airbnbs-market-and-regulations/

Park, G. (2022, November 21). *Airbnb vs. renting: which is more profitable for land-lords?* Liv.rent Blog. https://liv.rent/blog/landlords/airbnb-vs-renting-which-is-more-profitable/

Rusteen, D. (2020, July 16). *Vacation rental market research: Strategy and process*. OptimizeMyBnb. https://optimizemyairbnb.com/vacation-rental-market-research-strategy-process/

Shershikov, D. (2023, February 4). *Airbnb management fees: A complete breakdown of all the costs*. Awning. https://awning.com/post/airbnb-management-fees

Short-term rental market size to hit USD 315.18 Bn by 2033. (n.d.). Www.prece-denceresearch.com. https://www.precedenceresearch.com/short-term-rental-market

smartbnb. (2020, August 9). *Airbnb superhost status: Benefits of becoming one |* Hospitable. https://hospitable.com/airbnb-superhost-status-is-it-really-worth-it/

smartbnb. (2022, April 5). *Rental property maintenance: Guide for Airbnb hosts* Hospitable. https://hospitable.com/rental-property-maintenance/

Startup stories - Airbnb: A true rags to riches story. (2023, October 17). Startupsa-vant. https://startupsavant.com/startup-center/airbnb-origin-story

Understanding Airbnb Market Research | iGMS. (2023, June 22). IGMS. https:// www.igms.com/understanding-airbnb-market-research-for-vacation-rental-hosts-a-guide-to-success/#

Understanding Instant Book - Resource Center. (n.d.). Airbnb. https://www.airbnb. co.za/resources/hosting-homes/a/understanding-instant-book-17

What are response rate and response time and how are they calculated? - Airbnb help center. (n.d.). Airbnb. https://www.airbnb.co.za/help/article/430?locale=en& _set_bev_on_new_domain=1711223861_YzVjNWMxZmVlMTFh

What is an Airbnb superhost and how to become one. (n.d.). Hostaway. https://www. hostaway.com/blog/airbnb-superhost/

What legal and regulatory issues should I consider before hosting on Airbnb? - Airbnb help center. (n.d.). Airbnb. https://www.airbnb.co.za/help/article/376? locale=en&_set_bev_on_new_domain=1708277201_ZmQ4YTIwODFhZmJk

Zaidi, T. (n.d.). *What is Airbnb? [How it works, makes money, FAQ]*. TRVL-GUIDES. https://trvlguides.com/articles/what-is-airbnb

Image Reference

Angel, R. G. (2018, February 16). *Green stadium seats*. [Image] Unsplash. https://unsplash.com/photos/green-stadium-seats-KmKZV8pso-s

Arroyo, P. (2021, March 14). *White and black letter t print*. [Image] Unsplash. https://unsplash.com/photos/white-and-black-letter-t-print-_SEbdtH4ZLM

Barbhuiya, T. (2021, October 2). *A person stacking coins on top of a table*. [Image] Unsplash. https://unsplash.com/photos/a-person-stacking-coins-on-top-of-a-table-jpqyfK7GB4w

Cotten, J. J. (2021, January 25). *White and black animal on brown grass during daytime*. [Image] Unsplash. https://unsplash.com/photos/white-and-black-animal-on-brown-grass-during-daytime-8NmGOkPliE0

Davis, A. (2020, June 10). *White sofa set near window*. [Image] Unsplash. https://unsplash.com/photos/white-sofa-set-near-window-IWfe63thJxk

Distel, A. (2019, March 29). *Person reading book during daytime*. [Image] Unsplash. https://unsplash.com/photos/person-reading-book-during-daytime-Ej_GTF0JPss

Duffel, M. (2017, October 23). *Please stay on the path signage*. [Image] Unsplash. https://unsplash.com/photos/please-stay-on-the-path-signage-U5y077qrMdI

Garvey, E. (2020, July 6). *Text*. [Image] Unsplash. https://unsplash.com/photos/text-QoMQcDOadgk

Giovanella, F. A. (2020, October 14). *Person showing right middle finger*. [Image] Unsplash. https://unsplash.com/photos/person-showing-right-middle-finger-Lzys6r1xFD8

Holmes, A. (2020, May 10). *Brown brick house near green trees under blue sky during daytime*. [Image] Unsplash. https://unsplash.com/photos/brown-brick-house-near-green-trees-under-blue-sky-during-daytime-f6eWKcd8_dA

Janssens, E. (2017, September 30). *White planner with pen on top*. [Image] Unsplash. https://unsplash.com/photos/white-planner-with-pen-on-top-mO3s5xdo68Y

Lopes, H. (2019, March 23). *Man standing beside counter*. [Image] Unsplash. https://unsplash.com/photos/man-standing-beside-counter-QpjyqYy5R-U

Olloweb, A. (2018, January 19). *Magnifying glass near gray laptop computer*. [Image] Unsplash. https://unsplash.com/photos/magnifying-glass-near-gray-laptop-computer-d9ILr-dbEdg

Spiske, M. (2021, April 10). *Photos*. [Image] Unsplash. https://unsplash.com/photos/text-XrIfY_4cK1w

Tingey Injury Law Firm. (2020, May 13). *Brown wooden smoking pipe on white surface*. [Image] Unsplash. https://unsplash.com/photos/brown-wooden-smoking-pipe-on-white-surface-6sl88x150Xs

Unsplash+. (2022, September 13). *Unrecognizable mid-adults couple painting wall indoors at home relocation and DIY concept.* [Image] Unsplash. https://unsplash.com/photos/unrecognizable-mid-adults-couple-painting-wall-indoors-at-home-relocation-and-diy-concept-196ojVGVg2A

Unsplash+. (2023a, March 2). *A pink piggy bank sitting next to a stack of coins.* [Image] Unsplash. https://unsplash.com/photos/a-pink-piggy-bank-sitting-next-to-a-stack-of-coins-pSB8LM2NJds

Unsplash+. (2023b, April 14). *Checklist and notes written on paper a red tick and cartoon pencil on light-blue background concept of plans and schedule 3D rendering.* [Image] Unsplash. https://unsplash.com/photos/checklist-and-notes-written-on-paper-a-red-tick-and-cartoon-pencil-on-light-blue-background-concept-of-plans-and-schedule-3d-rendering-h1uertkV_wE

Unsplash+. (2023c, May 18). *A 3D image of the word web on a white surface.* [Image] Unsplash. https://unsplash.com/photos/a-3d-image-of-the-word-web-on-a-white-surface-qxQvB55QQLM

Wright, K. (2019, February 8). *Toddler looking at believe in yourself grafitti.* [Image] Unsplash. https://unsplash.com/photos/toddler-looking-at-believe-in-yourself-graffiti-yMg_SMqfoRU

Made in United States
Orlando, FL
29 December 2024

56677488R00104